OLDEST KANSAS CITY

KATY SCHAMBERGER

REEDY PRESS

Dedication

To my best husband and the other half of World's Finest, Rob Schamberger; our Missouri Tigers; my family, for cultivating my love of reading and writing; and Kansas City, my forever muse.

Reedy Press
PO Box 5131
St. Louis, MO 63139
reedypress.com

Library of Congress Control Number: 2025943629

ISBN: 9781681066097

Cover Design: Jill Halpin
Book Design: Linda Eckels

Cover photographs courtesy of KCPL and Hyer Boots.

Printed in the United States of America
25 26 27 28 29 5 4 3 2 1

TABLE OF CONTENTS

Day Trips

ACKNOWLEDGMENTS

Writing a travel guide is a collaborative effort, and I'm grateful to an unmatched network of people and resources to help me tell as complete, accurate, and engaging a story about Kansas City's history as possible.

My deepest gratitude to KCUR 89.3, Kansas City's NPR affiliate; and Kansas City Public Television's Flatland, two superb sources of reporting that were indispensable in my research and writing.

To the wonderful team behind the African American Heritage Trail of Kansas City: thank you for cultivating awareness of Kansas City's African American community, including the people and places that quite literally changed the trajectory of the city. Learn more at AAHTKC.org.

To the Visit KC team, especially Derek Byrne: thank you for your trust in me to tell Kansas City's stories. I'm part of your extended team for life.

To the Kansas City Public Library staff, especially the Central branch and the Missouri Valley Room: You were instrumental when I wrote my first book, and you proved just as vital during this second project. Thank you for your generosity in sharing so many rich historic photos.

I'm grateful to be supported by incredible family and friends who encourage my insatiable appetite for exploration and storytelling. Thank you also to everyone who granted time for interviews, fact-checking, and photo sharing throughout this process; to Pete Dulin, for editorial review; to Paul Andrews, for author photos that I will treasure forever; to the team at Reedy Press for guiding me through the process; to the local businesses that kept me caffeinated and fueled throughout this journey; and to Kima and Tikka, our two extraordinary cats who keep me loved and grounded.

Lastly, my sincere thanks to the Kansas City historians, explorers, and advocates who came first.

INTRODUCTION

It's easy to take history for granted, especially when something new and shiny captures our attention. And it's the new—or newish—that's put Kansas City on the map of the country's collective consciousness in the last two decades. A partial list? The new and expanding KC Streetcar, which now spans nearly 6.5 miles from the Missouri River to the University of Missouri–Kansas City; CPKC, home of the KC Current and North America's first soccer stadium built specifically for professional women's teams; the Moshe Safdie–designed Kauffman Center for the Performing Arts; and a built-from-the-ground-up, state-of-the-art airport terminal that opened in 2022.

Recent revitalization makes for a compelling comeback story, reclaiming buildings and neighborhoods from the scourge of neglect and disrepair to improve quality of life and equip Kansas City to host global events like the NFL Draft and FIFA World Cup 26™.

Yet you can't celebrate the present—or plan for the future—without acknowledging history. And Kansas City's legacy is a page-turner, the city's founding and growth intertwining (and often colliding) with significant historical events like the Civil War, forced Indigenous resettlement, World War I, and Prohibition, among others.

Rakish criminals, corrupt political bosses, ruthless Mafia members, innovative inventors, fearless explorers, outspoken advocates, savvy entrepreneurs—Kansas City's cast of characters is as intriguing as any Hollywood blockbuster, and you'll meet many of them in the pages of this book.

Just as fascinating is the list of things created in and around Kansas City: Bomb Pop popsicles, sliced bread, Hydrox cookies, Hallmark cards, Teflon pans, the Happy Meal, Russell Stover chocolates, the Crock-Pot, and the McRib.

It's here, in the heart of America, that a bluff-top, riverfront settlement grew into a bistate metropolitan area that includes

14 counties and a 2024 population of more than 2.2 million people. *Oldest Kansas City* will take you through much of this metropolitan area to better understand the people and places that have shaped the city.

As with any sweeping narrative, the plot veers from triumph to tragedy: enduring landmarks built by enslaved peoples, a desperate fight led by three sisters to protect an Indigenous burial ground from commercial development, racism, and segregation that simultaneously produced a vibrant and influential African American community in the 18th and Vine neighborhood while also enabling the predatory practices of structural racism, including redlining that turned bustling streets and lively communities into neighborhoods plagued by municipal neglect, poverty, and lower home values.

That's the roller coaster and responsibility of history: acknowledging and learning from harmful practices while also identifying and celebrating growth, progress, and inclusion. I've written about Kansas City for more than two decades—in a previous travel guide, in regional and national magazines, and for travel and tourism organizations. Yet it was while writing *Oldest Kansas City* that I truly grasped the gravity of the writer's role: History demands responsibility, humility, and curiosity—a willingness to ask hard questions and share not just an informed perspective but also a comprehensive one.

I have a new understanding and enthusiasm for this city, what it's endured, and what it's produced. Whether you're a lifelong Kansas Citian or visiting for the first time, the pages ahead are filled with adventure, discovery, and pro tips to make your adventure one to remember. You'll soon notice that the past is all around us and, with books like *Oldest Kansas City*, time travel is indeed possible.

Connect with @oldestkansascity on Instagram for more insider recommendations and upcoming events, and to share your historic Kansas City discoveries. As Wilbert Harrison first sang in 1959, "We're goin' to Kansas City . . . Kansas City, here we come!"

Kansas City, MO: Jackson, Clay, and Platte Counties

1946

Oldest Barbecue Restaurant

TIE!

Arthur Bryant's Barbeque

1727 Brooklyn Ave., Kansas City, MO

Gates B-B-Q

Locations vary, gatesbbq.com

If you want to start a heated and extensive debate while you're in Kansas City, pull a few residents aside and ask them one question: Who has better barbecue, Arthur Bryant's or Gates?

The original owners of both restaurants learned from the same person: Henry Perry, the rightful Barbecue King of Kansas City.

Perry, a Memphis native, arrived in Kansas City in 1907 and soon began selling barbecue meat from a small street-side stand in downtown Kansas City's Garment District. His proven technique: " . . . slow-cooked over a fire made from hickory and oak wood with the meat juices dripping directly on the coals," wrote Mackenzie Martin for KCUR.

As Martin explained, Perry was picky about his technique, but he'd grill (and sell!) anything, including possum and raccoon. Perry moved his business to a brick-and-mortar restaurant in the 18th and Vine neighborhood, where he employed several people, including Charlie Bryant. It was Charlie and Perry who worked in tandem to create Kansas City–style barbecue, which is sauce-focused.

Charlie's brother, Arthur, took over the business that Charlie had inherited from Perry when Charlie retired in 1946, and

Left: Gates B-B-Q table spread. Right: Arthur Bryant's spread. Photos courtesy of Visit KC

Arthur Bryant's Barbeque opened. Arthur's first order of business: " . . . tone down the barbecue sauce," Martin wrote. "According to what he told a reporter, Bryant thought 'Old Man Perry' and his brother had been overindulging in cayenne pepper for years."

That same year, George and Arzelia Gates bought a restaurant—Ol' Kentuck Bar-B-Q—at 19th and Vine and renamed it Gates Ol' Kentucky. Their son, Ollie, joined the family business while enrolled at Lincoln University in Jefferson City, Missouri. Ollie assumed leadership of the restaurant in 1960 and quickly grew it to multiple locations with an emphasis on cleanliness and service. Customers today are still greeted with the restaurant's signature opening: "Hi, may I help you?" (Pro tip: You better be ready to order; that line moves fast and means business! Step to the side if you need more time with the menu, or, when in doubt, always order burnt ends).

Bryant and Gates were both inducted in a 2021 ceremony to the American Royal's Barbecue Hall of Fame, joining Perry in their rightful place among barbecue royalty.

Honorable mention: Rosedale Bar-B-Q takes the title as the Kansas City area's oldest continuously operating barbecue restaurant (and it's family-owned, too), dating back to 1934. Visit the restaurant at 600 Southwest Blvd., Kansas City, Kansas.

——ca. late 1800s–WWII

OLDEST COLLECTION OF VICTORIAN HOMES

PENDLETON HEIGHTS

Cliff Dr. to Independence Ave., Chestnut Trafficway to Paseo, Kansas City, MO

Some sources call Pendleton Heights in Kansas City's Historic Northeast the oldest suburb in the city. The neighborhood is predated by the more centrally located Quality Hill; and, by early standards, you could make an argument that the Historic Northeast would be considered the first suburb, just minutes from the quickly growing Kansas City core.

Pendleton Heights, home to the Museum of Kansas City, offers several historic designations in its own right, including Kansas City's first boulevard—Independence Avenue—and the city's largest collection of true Victorian homes.

Let's briefly detour for a quick architecture lesson. Victorian architecture encompasses several styles, including the Gothic revival, Queen Anne, and Romanesque styles. This wide-ranging aesthetic had its heyday from 1830 to 1910 (during Queen Victoria's reign, naturally). Victorian homes typically combine Gothic architecture with details inspired by French, Italian, Tudor, and Egyptian design. Within Pendleton Heights you'll see some beautiful examples of Queen Anne homes, complete

Courtesy of Marelbu

with expansive porches, brightly colored exteriors, and ornate trim.

Pendleton Heights is located about 10 minutes northeast of downtown Kansas City and is bounded by Independence Avenue to the south, Chestnut Trafficway to the east, and the Paseo to the west. The neighborhood's northern border is comprised of cliffs, which spawned one of the most picturesque routes in Kansas City: a four-mile stretch of scenic byway called Cliff Drive, now open only to pedestrian traffic. As you take in panoramic views while perched above the East Bottoms and the Missouri River, you might just feel like one of those early explorers who recognized so much potential in this riverfront area.

Honestly, you could spend a full and enriching day just exploring Pendleton Heights. One of the most beloved examples of Victorian residential architecture is Tiffany Castle, located at 100 Garfield. The solid stone castle was built in 1908 by Dr. Flavel B. Tiffany, an eye doctor who wanted to build a home reminiscent of the European castles that so captured his imagination. The castle joins a number of other Victorian homes built between the late 1800s and World War II.

"The architecture here is, for the most part, pretty stellar," said Pendleton Heights resident Linda Fleischman in a 2022 article published in the *Northeast News*. Fleischman moved to the neighborhood from New York and has since become a dedicated board member of the Pendleton Heights Neighborhood Association. "We've been here for more than 15 years and I love it."

Pro tip: Fuel up for your Pendleton Heights adventure at a favorite neighborhood hangout, PH Coffee (2200 Lexington Ave.) The coffee shop hosts all sorts of special events, from themed pop-up bars and kid-friendly story time to writers' groups and themed community conversations.

1857

Oldest Farmers Market

City Market

20 E 5th St., Kansas City, MO

Wandering through bustling crowds past rows of stocked, mostly open-air stalls during a warm weekend morning, it's hard to believe that City Market started as a single shed built atop the Missouri River bluffs in 1857.

Farmer Gabriel Prudhomme originally owned the land located near the confluence of the Kaw and Missouri Rivers. Eagle-eyed real estate speculator John McCoy teamed up with several partners to purchase the land.

Once the sale went through (a nine-year process), McCoy and his partners platted the Town of Kansas, named for the Kansa Indians. Part of that land—bordered by 4th, 5th, Walnut, and Main Streets—became what's known today as the City Market, surrounded by the River Market neighborhood.

"The City Market, which had been largely a farmers market, became one of the great agricultural emporiums of the United States, if not the world," wrote Dr. Ronald Miriani in Kansas City's City Market.

Subsequent decades saw a decline in the surrounding neighborhood and diminished retail as suburban grocery stores emerged. A renewed focus in the 1940s resulted in the complete bulldozing of the existing City Market, creating the pavilion-covered aisles that remain today.

Neglect continued to plague the City Market and its surrounding River Market neighborhood. University of Missouri–Kansas City professor Marion A. Trozzolo purchased several historic buildings throughout the neighborhood, dubbing the area "River Quay" (pronounced "key"). Trozzolo

City Market spices

saw significant potential in the area as something similar to the French Quarter in New Orleans.

As more enterprising business owners purchased buildings in the neighborhood, members of the mafia took notice, too, and began opening adult-oriented businesses including bars and X-rated theaters.

A violent explosion rocked the River Quay in March 1977, destroying two businesses owned by the Bonadonna brothers. Subsequent bursts of violence broke out, and Fred Bonadonna would eventually join the witness protection program after testifying against two mob members.

Today, River Quay exists in name only, a colorful yet catastrophic chapter in the River Market's legacy. Ongoing development throughout the neighborhood sparked significant growth in the area's residential population, further aided by the opening of the Kansas City Streetcar in 2015.

After a trip through the weekend farmers market and City Market's perimeter shops, head less than one block south on Walnut Street and stop by Planters Seed & Spice Co. (513 Walnut St.), opened in 1924 by German immigrant Henry Wertheim. Planters continues to do a brisk business in seeds, spices, tea and coffee, and gardening supplies.

1950

Oldest-Operating Black-Owned Radio Station

KPRS 103.3

As you explore Kansas City, ditch your playlists and instead tune in to 103.3 FM. Known today as Hot 103 Jamz!, KPRS flooded local airwaves in 1950 as the first black-owned radio station west of the Mississippi.

US Army veteran Andrew "Skip" Carter pursued his passion for radio broadcasting once his service ended, studying at the RCA Institute for Electronics and New York University. He had dual dreams of being on-air and also leading a radio station committed to black artists. In that era of segregation, Carter couldn't make any headway on the East Coast and instead began selling radio ad time in Chicago.

A letter by Carter published in *Broadcast* magazine condemning racism within the FCC caught the attention of former Kansas governor Alf Landon, who brought Carter to the area to run one of his stations in Leavenworth. Landon helped Carter secure his FCC license in 1949; he was only the second black man to receive such a license.

Carter, equipped with a transmitter given to him by Landon, started KPRS-AM in Kansas City with the help of his wife, Mildred Rhone. At her prompting in the 1960s, Carter applied for an FM license and KPRS-FM went on-air in 1963.

In the decades since, KPRS and other Carter Broadcast Group stations have offered a mix of music and community-focused programming like "Voices from Midtown" and "Generation Rap." That focus on community involvement and advocacy continues today. One example in recent years: a programming initiative, "Put the Guns Down KC," which changed traditional, station-identifying openings to direct calls to action that encourage safe conflict resolution and the sharing of crime-solving information.

The station's music and familial lineage also continues. The Carters' grandson, Mike Carter, started his broadcast career at just 8 years old with a jazz-focused program called the *Mike Lewis Show* (Lewis is Mike's middle name). Mike assumed leadership of the Carter Broadcast Group in 1987, maintaining the company's family ownership. Today, Hot 103 Jamz! is the city's hip-hop and R&B go-to, part of a portfolio of radio stations that include gospel- and R&B-focused broadcasts.

Fun fact: Carter Broadcast Group cofounder Andrew "Skip" Carter took his well-deserved place in the Chicago-based Radio Hall of Fame in a 1995 induction ceremony.

Andrew "Skip" Carter. Courtesy of Carter Broadcast Group

1951

Oldest Original Pork Tenderloin Sandwich Recipe

Kitty's Cafe

810 ½ E 31st St., Kansas City, MO

The pork tenderloin sandwich at Kitty's Cafe may be among the earliest examples of fusion cuisine in Kansas City.

Paul Kawakami and his wife, Kitty, moved to Kansas City and opened the casual eatery in 1951 after having spent time in a World War II internment camp. They had the idea to infuse a traditional pork tenderloin sandwich with Japanese flavors, opting to coat thin slices of pork tenderloin in a panko breading, which adds a craveable crunch, and stack them three high on a soft, lightly toasted bun.

"It's hard to find the perfect pork tenderloin that is soft and not too chewy and perfectly seasoned and a little bit crunchy and this has all those things," wrote longtime Kansas City restaurant critic Charles Ferruzza, who passed away in 2020.

Pork tenderloin from Kitty's Cafe

Although the restaurant changed ownership several times since the Kawakamis opened it, it has remained in Asian American hands. Today, Charlie Soulivong and his daughter, Jinna, are in charge. When Kitty's

Cafe reopened in fall 2024 after a planned renovation to revive the café lobby and kitchen took months longer than scheduled, customers lined up around the block to get their sandwich fix.

The best way to order a Kitty's Cafe pork tenderloin sandwich? With a side of tater tots and plenty of homemade hot sauce. (If you're not into pork, try a tenderloin made with a crispy catfish or chicken fillet. Still—don't skip the hot sauce.)

Early risers also flock to Kitty's Cafe for a menu that includes breakfast sandwiches, including the ultimate trifecta: egg, bacon, and sausage. The menu is simple—burgers, BLTs, and a classic grilled cheese round out the selection—and at the time of this writing, nothing on the menu is priced over $10. With more than 70 years of staying power, it's clear that Kitty's Cafe ownership knows what their customers want. And they deliver.

Pro tip: There's not much room inside the café, so plan to take your meal to go and enjoy it at your home or hotel, or snack as you explore the vibrant and charming 31st Street corridor. Head west to find delights such as Under the Cover, a romance bookstore; Urban Mining, an antique and vintage shop open the first weekend of each month; and Sister Anne's Records and Coffee, a beloved neighborhood hangout.

1887

Oldest Skyscraper

New York Life Building

9th and Walnut Sts., Kansas City, MO

Imagine this: It's the late 1880s, and Kansas City is bustling. Railroads now run along and over the river, rapidly expanding passenger and freight traffic. The nearby stockyards are doing a booming business in cattle and grain trade, housing is built as quickly as it can be, and the city's population exploded from 4,000 people in 1860 to 30,000 in the 1870s.

Downtown Kansas City—what's known today as the River Market and Central Business District neighborhoods—is also growing fast, as rapid economic development requires more office space. At the intersection of 9th and Baltimore Streets, an architectural wonder begins to emerge: the 10-story New York Life Building, Kansas City's first skyscraper (and its first building to include an elevator).

Built in 1887 and designed by New York–based McKim, Mead & White Architects, "this Neo-Renaissance Style office building symbolizes the faith of the moneyed East in Kansas City during the unprecedented prosperity of the 1880s," as written on the building's certified historical marker.

One of the Italianate-style building's most striking features is a bronze eagle poised for flight above the main entrance. The sculpture was created by Augustus Saint-Gaudens and joined a number of upscale finishing details, including a skylight-filled lobby, mosaic floors, cherry wood, and ornate marble. The building's construction is also an effective example of the economic ripple effect created by building booms. The "superstructure," as it was known at the time, required a significant amount of brick, but none could be found in the

Left: A historic view of the New York Life Building. Right: The New York Life Building, present day. Photos courtesy of KCPL

area. An enterprising duo, the Norcross Brothers, quickly built a brick plant at Third and Broadway to meet the sudden demand.

At the time of its opening, the New York Life Building had only a few neighbors and Baltimore Street remained bordered by tall cliffs that stretched just south from 9th to 11th streets. Nearby landmarks included the Hotel Cosby and Calvin W. Morton's Senate Saloon in a modest business district that encompassed just a dozen square blocks.

Today, the office building remains in use as administrative offices for the Roman Catholic Diocese of Kansas City–St. Joseph and Catholic Charities.

The New York Life Building is just down Baltimore Street from another city landmark: the Central Library branch of the Kansas City Public Library This quiet, tree-lined street makes for a lovely morning stroll, and nearby coffee shops and restaurants offer casual hangouts for food and drink. Travel south on Baltimore, then west on 10th Street, to see the library's famed parking garage that features a towering bookshelf facade.

2023

Oldest Black-Owned Brewery in Missouri

Vine Street Brewing

2010 Vine St., Bldg. 2A, Kansas City, MO

Compared to so many sites in this book, Vine Street Brewing Co. is a relative baby. Yet in the comprehensive history of Kansas City, this brewery's formation as the first black-owned brewing company to open in Missouri is a significant milestone.

Kansas City musician, advocate, and creative Kemet Coleman opened Vine Street Brewing on June 30, 2023, with the help of Head Brewers Woodie Bonds Jr. and Elliott Ivory and Director of Operations Annie McGinnis.

The brewery is a meaningful new chapter for a building with a rich history in Kansas City's 18th and Vine neighborhood. The 4,800-square-foot limestone structure originally housed the Street Department, one of Kansas City's first public works entities. As you explore the sprawling space equipped with a two-story taproom, brew room, and outdoor beer garden, you'll likely notice decades-old graffiti adorning some of the stone surfaces. Coleman wanted to keep this creative expression as part of the building's redesign, calling the location "sacred soil" in an interview with local NPR affiliate KCUR.

Courtesy of Vine Street Brewing

Coleman is adamant about Vine Street Brewing serving not just as a beer brewery but also as a hub for community events. That mentality aligns with 18th and Vine's long-standing role as a community hub. The neighborhood grew a self-sufficient community created in response to restrictions that prevented African American Kansas Citians from moving south of 27th Street in the first half of the 20th century.

"Black doctors, dentists and lawyers practiced and lived in the neighborhood while more than 600 businesses, hotels, theaters, restaurants, and stores flourished," according to information provided by the African American Heritage Trail of Kansas City. Here is where jazz music flourished and evolved, where baseball's Negro National League was created, where Kansas City barbecue thrived.

Vine Street Brewing Co. also pays homage to the history of beer itself. Among the first brewers: Egyptians, who produced beer in huge quantities to fuel the laborers who faced grueling conditions while building the pyramids of Giza.

"'When I first discovered that beer was an African invention, that really blew my mind,'" Coleman said in his KCUR interview. "'African women were essentially the first brewers.'"

Live music, bingo, community conversations—there's a good chance Vine Street Brewing will host an event that coincides with your visit. Check Vine Street's website, vinestbrewing.com, for an updated calendar and tap list.

1919

Oldest Active Black-Owned Newspaper

The Kansas City Call

1516 E 18th St., Kansas City, MO

The first issue of *The Kansas City Call* published on May 6, 1919, and *The Call* (founded by Chester A. Franklin) became one of the city's 22 newspapers published by the black community.

Franklin had moved to Kansas City six years prior from Denver, where he had assumed leadership of his father's newspaper business, the *Star*. Franklin realized that Kansas City had a larger black population than Denver, creating better opportunities to not only start but also grow a newspaper.

Franklin faced racial discrimination in much the same way that Carter Broadcast Group founder Andrew "Skip" Carter had when starting a Kansas City radio station. Kansas City's local printer's union barred its members from working with black editors, so Franklin had to teach himself how to work a typesetting machine in order to produce his publication.

A key hire—reporter Roy Wilkins in 1923—proved to be a turning point for the paper as Wilkins published

The Call's *office in Kansas City's 18th and Vine District*

A mural commemorates the founder of The Kansas City Call, *Chester Arthur Franklin.*

bold stories arguing against segregation and Jim Crow laws. "Wilkins also advocated against Franklin putting the most sensational and negative headlines on the front page of the newspaper," wrote Stuart Hoy and Glyne Gee in a retrospective published by Historic Missouri. "Wilkins believed that the front page should be strictly for positive news that would uplift the black community." (Fun fact: Wilkins went on to become executive secretary of the NAACP.)

This commitment to community coverage not only kept readers informed but also helped black Kansas Citians win local civil rights disputes. Two examples: the repeal of segregation laws in employment and housing, and securing the right for black people to serve on Kansas City juries.

After Franklin's death in 1955, his wife, Ada, and a business partner, Lucile Bluford, assumed leadership of *The Call.* Bluford's career at the newspaper spanned an incredible 69 years. Today, *The Call* maintains a weekly publication in addition to its digital site.

Lucile Bluford's legacy extends beyond her nearly seven decades with The Kansas City Call. *The University of Kansas journalism graduate also serves as the namesake for a Kansas City Public Library branch at 3050 Prospect Ave. that features an extensive collection of African American literature.*

1857

Oldest Neighborhood

Quality Hill

7th to 14th Sts., I-35 to Broadway, Kansas City, MO

Perched atop bluffs lining the Missouri River, Quality Hill is Kansas City's oldest continuously inhabited neighborhood.

Fur trader and businessman François Chouteau could be credited with sparking early development in Quality Hill. In 1821, Chouteau built Chouteau's Landing, a fur-trading post, on the southern side of the Missouri River before moving it to the north end of Troost Avenue five years later.

Fast-forward nine years, when a French priest—Father Benedict Roux—built Kansas City's first permanent church, St. John Francis Regis, at 11th and Pennsylvania Streets in Quality Hill. Chouteau's family, friends, and employees frequented the church, bringing pedestrian traffic to this hilltop location.

It was this activity, combined with Quality Hill's scenic overlook, that prompted visitor Kersey Coates to purchase a sizable amount of land within Quality Hill in 1857. Coates, a Pennsylvania native, envisioned an upscale residential neighborhood located near the bustling riverfront and market but far enough (and high enough) to avoid flooding and the general muck and bustle of the Stockyards.

Former Kansas City Mayor Dr. Johnston Lykins quickly built a mansion that same year, and Coates followed suit in 1859. After the Civil War, Quality Hill saw a building boom in the 1880s that introduced a number of stately Victorian homes and several churches—Immaculate Conception, Grace and Holy Trinity Cathedral, and the Swedish Evangelical Lutheran Church among them. Quality Hill also expanded to include

Quality Hill Progress Club. Courtesy of KCPL

several upscale hotels and the Progress Club, built in 1893 as a social club for the city's prominent Jewish families.

Less than three decades later, that building boom didn't just slow; it abruptly fizzled. Wealthy Quality Hill residents could no longer stand the smell of the West Bottoms' meatpacking houses. And although many of the homes were relatively new, the Victorian architecture required expensive upkeep. Many residents headed south, populating a growing number of Kansas City suburbs. The empty mansions were subdivided into multifamily configurations like apartments, flats, and rooming houses.

Today, Quality Hill remains a popular destination for downtown multifamily living and a home to an eclectic mix of retail businesses and restaurants, including the Peanut, which opened in the early 1930s as a speakeasy and remains open today as Kansas City's oldest bar and grill (and one of several Peanut locations throughout the metro. Pro tip: Get the wings.).

1899

Oldest East–West Boulevard

Independence Avenue

Kansas City, MO

Kansas City's extensive array of fountains tends to attract most of the architectural acclaim, but the city's role as a leader in the development of parks and boulevards is equally impressive.

As Patrick Alley and Dona Boley wrote in *Images of America: Kansas City's Parks and Boulevards*, plans to create an extensive and eye-catching system of parks and boulevards was the result of collaboration among a newspaper editor, a prominent businessman, an attorney, a landscape architect, and an increasingly powerful political boss (quite the combo!).

A historic view of Independence Avenue. Courtesy of KCPL

Here's some perspective: Nearly 25,000 people called Kansas City home in 1869. That number jumped to 55,000 people in 1880, then doubled just 10 years later to 119,668 residents in 1890. Railroads, steamboats, shipping, stockyards, and storefronts don't always make for picturesque surroundings.

A flurry of advocacy (and a fair amount of fighting and setbacks) led to the creation of Kansas City's Parks Board in 1892, led by board president August Robert Meyer. Meyer's travels throughout the US and Europe made him a staunch supporter of municipal beautification. Meyer partnered with landscape architect George Kessler to write and publish the 1893 Report of the Board of Park and Boulevard Commissioners. Not only was the report an illuminating examination of city topography, population, and growth, but it also served as the city's urban design blueprint, the forebear of urban planning as we know it today.

Despite this thorough document that clearly outlined next steps, Kansas City lacked funding for any park or boulevard projects. Multiple battles ensued at the ballot box, bringing with them petitions, lawsuits, and public meetings. Finally, in 1900, a Missouri Supreme Court decision extinguished the anti-park fight, and the Kansas City parks and boulevard system was completed in the 1920s.

This inspirational starting point of the nationwide City Beautiful movement included five boulevards, starting with Independence Avenue (which Meyer called home). This 0.96-mile stretch of boulevard spanned Woodland Avenue to Benton Boulevard and was completed in 1899.

Around 1914, homes along Independence Avenue began to be replaced by businesses and heavier commercial traffic. It's more difficult today to envision Independence Avenue's aesthetic beginnings compared to other city boulevards that retain more of their initial design—Ward Parkway is a prime example. And in the history books, Kansas City will forever be at the forefront of beautification-focused urban planning.

"The original 1893 plan, implemented by George Kessler, brought the idea of urban beauty to a reality not demonstrated as completely in any other American city," wrote Alley and Boley in *Images of America: Kansas City's Parks and Boulevards*. "Kansas City became famous for its beautiful vistas and parkways and served as a model for other communities as the City Beautiful movement spread across the nation."

A visit to Independence Avenue puts you in close proximity to other destinations mentioned in this book, including the historic Pendleton Heights and Scarritt Renaissance neighborhoods. Independence Avenue also hosts a mouthwatering array of carnicerias like San Antonio Meat Market, a tasty lunch stop.

1887

Oldest-Operating Retail Business

Browne's Irish Market

3300 Pennsylvania Ave., Kansas City, MO

Not only is Browne's Irish Market the oldest still-operating retail business in Kansas City, but it's also the oldest Irish business in the world outside of Ireland.

Irish immigrants Ed and Mary Flavin started Flavin's Market at 27th and Jefferson Streets in 1887. The ideal location positioned the market about halfway between the bustling Missouri riverfront and the thriving Westport neighborhood. From this modest storefront in front of their family home, the Flavins sold food, wares, and "Irish hospitality to their many customers and friends," as detailed on Browne's website.

Brisk business prompted the Flavins to build a new store—the present-day location of Browne's Irish Market at 33rd and Pennsylvania Streets, open since 1901. The Flavins' daughter, Margaret, and her husband, James, began running the store in 1915, continuing a family lineage that perseveres today.

When so many businesses collapsed during the Great Depression, Browne's hung on, thanks in part to a generous policy that allowed customers to pay what they could. After all, Browne's is much more than a retail store (and also a restaurant—more on that in a moment). It's a gathering place, a neighborhood hub where the Brownes watch families grow just as theirs did.

Browne's Irish Market on St. Patrick's Day

In the late 1980s, Kerry Browne (granddaughter of James Flavin) and her husband, John McClain, assumed ownership of the store, and they operate it today. The sprawling interior layout expanded in 2008 to include six rooms of Irish and Celtic gifts. And in the store's main front room, a deli and bar do a brisk business, especially in the weeks preceding the Kansas City St. Patrick's Day Parade, the nation's third-largest parade held on March 17. On parade morning, crowds begin gathering before sunrise to fuel up on hearty Irish breakfast sandwiches and Irish coffee before continuing a few blocks east to Broadway, the parade's primary thoroughfare through Kansas City's Midtown and Westport neighborhoods.

It's easy to be distracted by the food and drink at Browne's, but the retail selection is just as memorable. Irish-made gifts, including pottery, lace, and hand-tooled leather, are in abundance, not to mention an impressive selection of Irish-themed apparel. Whiskey lovers, take note: George Vial is an Irish whiskey educator for Browne's and has cultivated one of the area's most diverse selections of Irish whiskies, as he explained in a 2022 story for local NPR affiliate KCUR.

If you do stop by to raise a glass, don't forget the traditional Irish toast, "Slainte!"—pronounced "slawn-che."

Pro tip: If you plan on a meal at Browne's, check the deli hours before you go. Food is typically sold from 10 a.m. to 5 p.m., Thursday through Saturday. Not sure what to order? Get a Reuben and savor every bite.

1856/1991

Oldest and Largest Collection of Pre–Civil War Artifacts

The Arabia Steamboat Museum

400 Grand Blvd., Kansas City, MO

The steamboat *Arabia*, one of approximately 400 steamboats that sank in the often-perilous waters of the Missouri River, is one of the more compelling—and often overlooked—exhibits detailing 19th-century life in and around Kansas City.

On a September day in 1856, the steamboat *Arabia* had set sail with more than 200 tons of cargo bound for general stores and homes throughout the Midwest, near what's known today as Parkville, when it hit an underwater tree snag. All of the more than 100 passengers were successfully rescued from the wreckage.

There are numerous stories of the Missouri River's changing course impacting lives and livelihoods throughout the Kansas City area, and the *Arabia* is one such example.

"Due to erosion, the Missouri River changed course over time, and the *Arabia* was buried underground for over a century—along with all of its precious cargo," according to the museum. "Lying 45 feet deep beneath a Kansas cornfield, the *Arabia*'s payload was protected from light and oxygen, and, thus, was remarkably well-preserved."

Treasure hunter Bob Hawley, along with his sons, David and Greg, used maps and a metal detector to locate the wreckage

Left photo courtesy of Visit KC. Right photo courtesy of the Arabia Steamboat Museum

under a Kansas cornfield in 1987. With permission from the landowner, Hawley's crew began to recover the *Arabia* in 1988, an intensive, monthslong process involving a crane and nearly two dozen irrigation pumps that helped unearth an incredible array of artifacts, from clothing and tools to weaponry and, if you can believe it, green sweet pickles that were still edible. Further evidence of the boat's airtight preservation: Crates of fine china were discovered, still nestled among crisp, dry yellow straw as if it had been packed just weeks before, rather than a century and a half ago.

The Arabia Steamboat Museum opened in 1991, part of the River Market's bustling City Market area. The museum's location, where Kansas City's original development began, is especially fitting; you can explore the steamboat's preserved cargo and structure, then step outside and shop the city's oldest farmers market.

Museum staff recommends at least 90 minutes for a full, self-guided tour throughout the museum and its artifacts, a find so important that Visit KC says it's been called "the King Tut's Tomb of the Missouri River."

1910/1939

Oldest Museum Building in Kansas City

The Museum of Kansas City

3218 Gladstone Blvd., Kansas City, MO

Lumber baron Robert Alexander Long (commonly referred to as "R.A.") built a four-story mansion called Corinthian Hall in 1910, just one part of a widespread construction legacy throughout the Kansas City area that included a downtown office building, the Liberty Memorial, and Lee's Summit's Longview Farm, a 1,780-acre farm that *The Kansas City Star* once called "a rural Versailles."

Local architectural guidebook *Kansas City: A Place in Time* calls Corinthian Hall "probably the most notable example of Beaux Arts Classicism in the city. The entire complex achieves harmony through uniformity in its red tile roofs, Bedford limestone facing, and repetition of design elements and details."

It's hard to believe that a mere family of four lived in this 34,000-square-foot mansion—and perhaps the sprawling estate proved too much for some of the family to manage. After R.A. and his wife, Ella, died, their daughters, Sallie and Loula, donated the mansion and the surrounding land in 1939 to the Kansas City Museum Association for the express purpose of transforming the palatial home into a public museum.

Over the next nearly eight decades, the Kansas City Museum (originally a science museum) operated out of the massive space before relocating to Union Station; the Kansas City Museum continued operations, shifting its focus to serve as a humanities-centered city museum. Yet the passage of time—and so much consistent foot traffic—took its toll on Corinthian Hall,

which closed in 2017 for a multiyear restoration and rehabilitation.

A jubilant group of museum staff and supporters gathered in October 2021 to celebrate the reopening of the museum, which was rebranded as the Museum of Kansas City in early 2025. The thorough and extensive renovation of Corinthian Hall carried a price tag of $22 million, and as Chiluba Musonda, deputy director of operations, said in an interview with KCUR, it took a huge number of people to accomplish.

"'Over a thousand hands have touched this building in terms of the work, from electricians to plumbers to guys who work on the HVAC system,'" he said.

The three-story building includes a variety of exhibits that explore various facets of Kansas City's development and culture. You'll learn more about the Long family's daily life in Corinthian Hall on the first floor, while the second floor details the history of the city. The third floor presents a balanced look at Kansas City's past, present, and future. Don't miss "A Cultural & Community Restoration: 1970s to Present Day," a deep dive into the neighborhoods and populations that comprise the Historic Northeast.

One of the Museum of Kansas City's hidden gems is Elixir, a replica soda fountain that operates in the museum's basement. Classic refreshments like phosphates and milkshakes are served alongside baked goods, a full coffee bar, and a small cocktail menu.

1933

Oldest Fried-Chicken Restaurant

Stroud's

5410 NE Oak Ridge Dr., Kansas City, MO

Stroud's Restaurant opened in 1933 as a barbecue restaurant at 85th Street and Troost Avenue. When beef became difficult to buy as a result of World War II rationing, owners Guy and Helen Stroud decided to shift the menu's focus to pan-fried chicken. (Fun fact: At that time, an original chicken dinner cost $0.35!)

That chicken soon put Stroud's on the map, as did another menu item: cinnamon rolls.

"Growing up in Kansas City in the 1980s, I ate my fair share of conventional cinnamon rolls," recounts Gina Kaufman on an episode of her *Real Humans* podcast. "But the cinnamon roll that spoke to me most was the one they served at Stroud's, where baskets of buttery dinner rolls covered in cinnamon sugar glaze arrived at the table with every meal."

Food GPS blogger Joshua Lurie's verdict? "They were easily the best cinnamon rolls I'd eaten, ever."

Stroud's changed hands in 1977 when two Kelly's Westport Inn bartenders, Mike Donegan and Jim Hogan, bought the restaurant. They brought two of Helen's cooks and a number of recipes with them, then finessed the Stroud's menu that's still served today.

You might not associate a traditional pan-fried chicken meal, complete with mashed potatoes and gravy, green beans, and, of course, cinnamon rolls, with fine dining, but Stroud's trophy case says otherwise. The restaurant received a James Beard

Award for Excellence, which former *Kansas City Star* food editor Jill Wendholt Silva likened to "the culinary equivalent of an Oscar." They've also scooped up a Zagat Award for Best Restaurant, have been featured on the Food Network's *The Best Thing I Ever Ate* and in the pages of *The New York Times*, *Gourmet* magazine, *The Wall Street Journal*, and *Playboy* magazine.

Although the original Stroud's location closed as a result of eminent domain, a Northland restaurant operates in an expanded 1829 log cabin and farmhouse known as event venue Oak Ridge Manor, also owned by Donegan, Hogan, and Donegan's brother, Dennis.

You can't beat the experience of dining at Stroud's, but if you're feeling brave and want to test your culinary skills, local TV station WDAF published a recipe for the restaurant's signature pan-fried chicken. Find it at fox4kc.com/mornings/recipes-strouds-pan-fried-chicken.

Original Stroud's. Courtesy of KCPL

1821–1865

Oldest-Remaining Wagon Tracks

Minor Park

11103 Holmes Rd., Kansas City, MO

When you consider weather, construction, and the general pace of change that occurs over two centuries, it's remarkable that original wagon tracks (also known as "swales") are still visible. As pointed out in *Kansas City: A Place in Time*, the still-existing swales are a testament to the tremendous amount of wagon traffic that passed through the area as travelers flocked to the Santa Fe Trail. "Luckily, the swales in Minor Park offer the curious an opportunity to look at the lasting marks that the age of the horse-drawn wagon left on the face of Kansas City."

The topography at this particular section of trail may have played a role, too. According to a park summary by the National Park Service, Minor Park included a crossing at the Blue River. Once wagons forded the river, they had to be pulled up a hill and "muddied, eroded, and rutted the trail as they climbed this rise."

The Santa Fe Trail is mentioned several times throughout this book, so let's pause for a bit of trail-specific context. The Santa Fe Trail connected Missouri with Santa Fe, New Mexico, and was pioneered by Missouri trader William Becknell, who began his trek from Franklin, Missouri, in 1821. Travelers before Becknell had frequently been arrested by Spanish soldiers as they approached Santa Fe. By the time Becknell arrived, however, Mexico had overthrown its Spanish rule and the new government eagerly welcomed trade. The Santa Fe Trail

Minor Park wagon swales. Courtesy of Wikimedia Commons

continued to operate as a busy commercial thoroughfare until it was replaced by a railroad route managed by the Atchison, Topeka and Santa Fe Railway.

Although railroads would fully eclipse the Santa Fe Trail in 1880, wagon traffic had started declining years before. The last large-scale wagon train left Kansas City in the spring of 1866.

A paved road through Minor Park now makes for easy access to the swales. An abundance of recreation awaits, too, including a playground, the Blue River Greenway Trail, and Minor Park Golf Course. If you want to literally leave your mark on the park, bring a padlock to affix to the Old Red Bridge (or buy one at the Minor Park Golf Course pro shop), the first iteration of which was built in 1859.

If you're passionate about swale sighting, add another nearby stop to your list. Swales are still visible near the New Santa Fe Cemetery at 900–902 West Santa Fe Trail Road, about a 10-minute drive west from Minor Park.

2025

OLDEST MUSEUM OF BARBECUE

MUSEUM OF BBQ

2450 Grand Blvd., Kansas City, MO

Houston and Memphis may have something to say about it, but honestly, where else would you put the world's first museum dedicated to barbecue?

Inside downtown Kansas City's Crown Center (details in the sidebar), the Museum of BBQ opened in spring 2025 to offer an artistic and informative view of barbecue: its elements, various regions of American barbecue, and the technical process, to start.

Museum founder Jonathan Bender is no stranger to the world of barbecue. His career as a food writer and author has led him down a delicious path, with stops as a judge at the American Royal World Series of Barbecue and as founder of the Kansas City food publication *Recommended Daily*, "all in pursuit of learning more about what Kansas Citians eat and drink," according to Bender's bio.

Bender's hands-on experience in the local culinary scene helped ensure an interactive museum experience that entertains as it educates.

"This is a place where barbecue comes alive," Bender said in a museum press release. "We want you to play and learn and come away with an appreciation for the joy of community that is part of barbecue culture."

To bring the museum to life, Bender teamed up with Kansas City chef and restaurateur Alex Pope, butcher and co-owner of Local Pig butcher shop in the City Market. Note: If you're souvenir shopping for someone who loves food, don't miss a stop by Local Pig and lunch at the adjoining sandwich shop, Pigwich.

Just how omnipresent is barbecue in Kansas City? The metro area is home to more than 100 local barbecue restaurants and countless competitions. Each fall, barbecue's best of the best (around 500 teams from around the world) fire up their grills and smokers at the American Royal, the world's biggest barbecue contest. Details available at americanroyal.com.

The Museum of BBQ's location inside Crown Center adds another dimension to this dining, shopping, lodging, and business destination. The Crown Center complex is home to Hallmark Cards HQ, featuring Kaleidoscope, a kid-friendly makerspace; SEA LIFE Kansas City Aquarium; LEGOLAND Discovery Center; and Halls, the upscale department store envisioned by Hallmark Cards. Get a complete directory at crowncenter.com.

The Museum of BBQ features a bean pit filled with 8,000 "beans." Jump in!

1894

OLDEST GOLF COURSE

KENWOOD GOLF LINKS

Intersection of 36th St. and Gillham Rd.

An historic marker and a partial stone wall are all that remain of the city's first golf course, but it's a sight worth seeing. In 1894, an enterprising group of Scottish residents created the Kenwood Golf Links, a nine-hole course that spanned 36th to 38th Streets and Gillham (Oak) Road to Charlotte Street.

The links were part of the Hyde Park Country Club, the city's first country club, and the course was the 17th to be built in the US after golf arrived as a sport in 1888.

In a story about the course written for the *Martin City Telegraph*, Diane Euston cites a description of Kenwood Golf Links from one of Hyde Park Country Club's first members, William D. McLeod.

"There were no bunkers, but there were 'enough natural hazards' to make the nine-hole course difficult," Euston wrote. "The putting greens were in anything but stellar condition, and the only time the grass was ever cut was 'when some ambitious player brought his own lawn mower out and personally performed the work.'"

Added *Kansas City Star* reporter Henry Van Brunt, in a story cited by authors Bruce Mathews and Stephen Mitchell in their book *Janssen Place*: "The fairways were all 'rough' and the greens were strictly improvised. The ninth hole was the original rim-sunk tin can under a big linden tree on the Van Brunt lawn where the elements of putting were taught." Golfers also had to watch for roving cattle from nearby Westport until a newly passed herd law kept animals corralled in pastures.

Courtesy of the Historical Marker Database

Fire would consume the Hyde Park clubhouse just one year after it opened. With the golf course quickly growing in popularity, Hyde Park members reorganized as the Kansas City Country Club and opened at what's now Loose Park in 1896, spanning 51st to 55th Streets west of Wornall Road (and just south of the Country Club Plaza, Kansas City's first suburban shopping district).

Today, the sprawling terrain of Gillham Park, original site of the Hyde Park Country Club, remains a recreational destination for the vibrant neighborhoods that surround the park, named for Robert Gillham, "the father of Kansas City's cable railway system," according to the Kansas City Parks and Recreation Department. Explore the park on any given day and, weather permitting, you'll see anything from flag football and pickleball to baseball and soccer.

This bustling part of Kansas City's Midtown makes for a picturesque stroll. See the Kenwood Golf Links historic marker, explore Gillham Park and, if you're an architectural enthusiast, head to nearby 36th Street and Janssen Place. Here, you'll find the one-street Janssen Place neighborhood, home to 19 carefully preserved mansions built in the early 1900s, many by Kansas City lumber barons.

1856

Oldest Antebellum Home

Alexander Majors House

8201 State Line Rd., Kansas City, MO

When Alexander Majors built his family home in 1856, State Line Road was merely a dirt path that wound from Westport Landing to the Santa Fe Trail. According to the Wornall/Majors House Museums, Majors carefully selected his home's location—including the direction it faced—before construction began.

"Majors deliberately built his home mere feet from what was then the national border of the U.S., symbolically looking westward. His house's strategic location enabled him to conduct business on leased property in the Kansas territory. On this leased property, Majors had huge corrals, grazing lands, oxen pens, barns, and wagon and blacksmith shops. Family legend has it that Majors did this because goods in the Territory were not taxed, making him a very shrewd businessman."

Majors's résumé included founding the Pony Express and helping to establish the Kansas City Stockyards. His family's home—likely built mostly by enslaved people—is a T-shaped structure built as a freehand version of a Greek Revival–style farm home. Majors opted to build his home with wood instead of brick and also equipped the home with a feature unusual for the time: a two-story recessed front porch.

The home remained in the Majors family until 1904, then was purchased by the Ruhl family, who made several additions to the house, including a new two-story section that added two rooms and an indoor kitchen.

After the Majorses' farmstead was sold and divided in 1924 to make room for suburban housing development, the mansion became a schoolhouse. Developers considered demolishing the home, but its all-wood construction made it too sturdy (translation: too expensive) to raze.

Louisa Johnston, Alexander Majors's great-granddaughter, bought the crumbling mansion in 1930 and began a slow but steady restoration process. Johnston's longtime friend, architect Terry Chapman, received the home in Johnston's will after her death in 1979. He completed a significant restoration and opened the home for tours in 1984, working with his wife, Victoria, to manage the house museum. In 2011, management of the house merged with that of another antebellum home located 3.5 miles away—the John Wornall House, built in 1858.

The Wornall/Majors House Museums offer a self-guided audio tour of Kansas City's Brookside neighborhood. The cost of the tour ($15) includes admission to the John Wornall House. Info: wornallmajors.org/walk.

Right: The Alexander Majors House includes an event space that's available for rent. Photos courtesy of the Wornall/Majors House Museums

1847

OLDEST BUILDING IN KANSAS CITY

KELLY'S WESTPORT INN

500 Westport Rd., Kansas City, MO

With its green and brick exterior and prominent lighted sign, it's hard to miss Kelly's Westport Inn, a longtime fixture at the corner of Pennsylvania Avenue and Westport Road. The Irish-themed bar opened in 1847 in what was originally known as the Albert G. Boone Store.

Today, Westport is best known around Kansas City as a nightlife district, a densely built neighborhood liberally peppered with bars, restaurants, and live music venues and surrounded by residential communities. In the city's early days—1833, to be exact—Westport was its own city, created when John Calvin McCoy opened a trading post on the opposite corner from where the Boone Store would be built (and which predated the Boone Store by 23 years).

Although Westport was several miles inland from the confluence of the Missouri and Kaw Rivers that prompted the creation of the Town of Kansas, the trading-focused community was ideally positioned as wagonloads of people set out on the nearby California, Oregon, and Santa Fe Trails. They'd stop in Westport to stock up on furs and goods at places like Boone Store, creating brisk business in the city.

Westport became even more infamous during the Civil War, when Kansas City's largest battle, the Battle of Westport, raged over an area that spans Westport to Loose Park (nearly 20 blocks). The "Gettysburg of the West" all but ended the

Civil War in the western states. Just before the turn of the century, Westport merged with the City of Kansas City.

Now—back to Kelly's, one of the city's most beloved watering holes. The Kelly family purchased the historic building in 1995, and Kelly's continues to draw crowds to its expansive, two-story interior that now includes a covered deck overlooking the surrounding neighborhood. Kelly's is, of course, a staple of the local Irish community and also serves as the unofficial meeting place for out-of-state sports watch parties, including Iowa State Cyclones alumni. It's one of the later-operating bars in the area, staying open until 3 a.m.

While you're there, look closely at the main bar for a Ten High whiskey bottle filled not with liquid, but with ashes. Those are the cremated remains of George Wiedenmann Sr., who owned the Boone building from 1903 until 1995.

Pro tip: There's no shortage of food options around Kelly's, but another local brand, Guy's Potato Chips, operates a deli and pizza shop in the back of the bar. Grab a giant slice or a freshly made sandwich and a bag of Guy's signature snack, manufactured just across the state line in Kansas City, Kansas, to make your visit even more quintessentially Kansas City

---

Right: A partial view of the bar's interior. Courtesy of Kelly's Westport Inn

1920

OLDEST BASEBALL LEAGUE FORMED IN KANSAS CITY

JOHN "BUCK" O'NEIL CENTER

The Paseo and 19th St., Kansas City, MO

There's a good reason that both the American Jazz Museum and the Negro Leagues Baseball Museum are under the same roof in Kansas City's 18th and Vine neighborhood. Both music and sport have played key roles in the growth and legacy of this, one of Kansas City's most historically significant neighborhoods.

Black baseball players began joining military, college, and company teams in the late 1800s. Players would occasionally "break through" to join white teams, most notably Moses Fleetwood Walker and Bud Fowler. Yet Jim Crow laws forced black players from any professional teams by 1900, so they countered by forming teams and "barnstorming" around the country to play any challengers who stepped up.

Several team owners, including Andrew "Rube" Foster, owner of the Chicago American Giants, met at the Paseo YMCA in 1920 to formally organize as the Negro National League. Kansas City's own Monarchs began to play in the

Buck O'Neil mural. Courtesy of Visit KC

league that same year, becoming one of the most successful baseball teams of all time. A who's who of baseball stardom all wore Monarchs uniforms at one point in their careers, including Satchel Paige, Jackie Robinson, Hilton Smith, Willard Brown, Ernie Banks, and Buck O'Neil.

O'Neil's history-making career—first as a baseball player, then as the first black person to coach in Major League Baseball when he joined the Chicago Cubs in 1962, and finally as the cofounder of the Negro Leagues Baseball Museum—has elevated him to icon status. The Paseo YMCA was renamed the Buck O'Neil Center. Bob Kendrick, president of the Negro Leagues Baseball Museum, is spearheading a capital campaign to revitalize the building, expanding archival and memorabilia displays and adding cutting-edge research and development capabilities like the NLBM Sports Science Center, dedicated to the math and science of baseball.

As for the Monarchs? They've experienced their own revitalization, taking the field in 2021 in place of the previously branded Kansas City T-Bones. The Monarchs have wasted no time in cementing their success, either, having won American Association of Professional Baseball league championships in 2021 and 2023.

In addition to the Buck O'Neil Center, don't miss a trip to the Negro Leagues Baseball Museum (1616 E 18th St.). If your trip coincides with baseball season, the Monarchs play at Legends Field in Kansas City, Kansas, part of a sports-centric development boom that resulted in nearby Children's Mercy Park, home of Sporting Kansas City, and NASCAR's Kansas Speedway.

1949

OLDEST STEAK HOUSE

THE GOLDEN OX

1600 Genessee St., Kansas City, MO

It's a bold proclamation in a city sometimes known as Cowtown, but the Golden Ox distinguishes itself as the local restaurant "where the steak was born."

The upscale steak house opened in the heart of Kansas City's Stockyards District in 1949. By this point, the district was far removed from its heyday in the early 1900s, when the Stockyards covered over 200 acres, employed 20,000 people, and consistently achieved a daily quota of 170,000 animals processed.

Still, the Stockyards would continue to operate until the 1990s. And in the meantime, the Golden Ox cultivated a reputation as a must-try steak house for both residents and visitors. The steak house operates on the first floor of the Livestock Exchange Building, a towering structure that helps set the tone for an outing steeped in history. Enter the dim, low-ceilinged restaurant and you immediately feel enveloped in a more glamorous era. A cozy bar is the perfect place to order a classic cocktail—a martini or a Manhattan, perhaps.

Let's get back to the Golden Ox's classification as the birthplace of steak. It's not as far-fetched as it might sound. This is the location that pioneered the city's signature steak, the Kansas City strip: a short loin cut served boneless.

An inspired and delicious reign came to an end when the Golden Ox closed its doors in 2014 due, in part, to a decline in West Bottoms neighborhood traffic when the new downtown entertainment venue, the T-Mobile Center, replaced the Golden Ox's neighbor, Kemper Arena, as the go-to for sporting events and concerts.

But wait! This story has a happy ending. Wes Gartner and Jill Meyers already owned Voltaire, another dim, cozy, historic West Bottoms haunt across the street from the Golden Ox. They purchased the steak house and reopened it in 2018. You know what they say: the more, the merrier. Gartner and Meyers reopened the Golden Ox with a new bar. The original remains in a 1950s addition to the Livestock Exchange building and is now home to Stockyards Brewery. Our recommendation? Enjoy a couple of local beers in the brewery's comfortable leather club chairs, then head down the hall for a dinner you won't soon forget. For bonus points, head to the other side of the West Bottoms neighborhood to see the world's largest cap gun at 1219 Union St., created by artist Brock Venti.

How's this for Cowtown trivia? In 1881, an Independence-based firm, Gudgell & Simpson, imported a Hereford Cornerstone sire from England. The sire, named Anxiety 4th, excelled at his job. Nearly all Hereford cattle in America are descended from this impressive specimen.

A partial view of the Golden Ox's dining room. Courtesy of the Golden Ox

1979

Oldest Happy Meal

Bernstein-Rein

4600 Madison Ave., Kansas City, MO

Yes, you read that title correctly. In the late 1960s, Kansas City advertising executive Bob Bernstein (founder of advertising agency Bernstein-Rein) signed all nine local McDonald's franchises. And they were in trouble.

Bernstein identified their first priority: children's marketing. ". . . because McDonald's in my mind, I thought it really appealed to children," Bernstein said in an interview with WDAF-TV celebrating Bernstein-Rein's 60-year milestone.

The start of the 1970s would see a flurry of promotions: a Styrofoam plane, followed by the Happy Cup, Happy Plate, Happy Lid, and Sippy Dipper Straw. Then, Bernstein took a cue from his son, Steve.

"I would read the same cereal box over and over again, and it was true, he was frustrated with me, he'd say, 'Don't you have something better to read?'" Steve said in the same WDAF-TV interview.

That's when it clicked for Bernstein: Kids enjoy an activity while they're eating. And so the colorful, highly visual Happy Meal boxes were born. The first design? Circus wagons. Early toys tucked into the Happy Meal included small toys like erasers. The kids-themed meals launched in 1979, and four years later, Bernstein sold the Happy Meal patent to McDonald's for a crisp $1.

"When I came up with the idea, I never dreamed that it would be what it is today," Bernstein told WDAF-TV.

Bob Bernstein with a Happy Meal box. Courtesy of Treasure Advertising

Among Bernstein's keepsakes? A Bronze Happy Meal, gifted to him by McDonald's Corporation in 1987. The box is inscribed: "Thank you for bringing the Happy Meal, a bold idea, to the McDonald's system. Your insight and conviction truly has made McDonald's a fun place for children for the past 10 years."

Should you find yourself at a Kansas City–area McDonald's location and you order a Happy Meal, it's no stretch to say you're purchasing a piece of history. Save the box!

In addition to founding the advertising agency Bernstein-Rein, Bob Bernstein also created Beauty Brands, retail locations that are part salon, part spa, and part beauty supply store. To learn more about Bernstein and other notable Kansas City marketing and advertising leaders, check out the Kansas City Marketing Legends *podcast.*

1946

Oldest Science-Focused Library

Linda Hall Library

5109 Cherry St., Kansas City, MO

There's no shortage of businesses and organizations that occupy historic homes throughout Kansas City, and the Linda Hall Library is one of them.

Upon Linda Hall's passing, Linda and her husband, Herbert, bequeathed $6 million with these instructions: "establish a free public library for the use of the people of Kansas City and the public generally," as detailed on the library's website. The Halls didn't specify a particular type of library that should be created, only that it would be housed on the grounds of their 1913 estate, located on 15 acres south of the Country Club Plaza (now part of the University of Missouri–Kansas City campus).

Led by Herbert's cousin and business partner, Paul D. Bartlett Sr., the library's first board of trustees decided to focus the library on science and its history, and it opened in 1946.

"Over the years, the library has acquired a world-class collection of books, including original works of scientists such as Galileo, Darwin, and Einstein," according to UMKC.

The Halls' estate was demolished in 1964 and the library structure as it exists today was built. Now, the Linda Hall Library "collects materials in 82 languages and is widely known for the breadth and

depth of its collections, its role as an international destination for research and scholarship, its support of teachers of STEM curriculum, and the vast resources it provides to learners of all ages who wish to embark on journeys of scientific exploration," as detailed by the library.

Rotating exhibitions offer a deeper dive into specific areas of science. In 2025, for example, the library hosted a cookbook retrospective, "Follow the Recipe," that examined the cookbook as a cultural artifact reflective of social dynamics, economic conditions, and evolving palates. A second exhibit, "Life Beyond Earth?" explored the age-old question and created an interactive environment in which library visitors could conduct their own search. Check lindahall.org for an updated events calendar as you plan your visit.

Travel tip: The Linda Hall Library is a 10-minute walk from the National Museum of Toys and Miniatures—those two stops make for a Kansas City adventure to remember. Or create a fully science-themed itinerary with a stop at the Linda Hall Library followed by a visit to Union Station to explore the planetarium and interactive museum, Science City funded and led by Kansas City–based engineering firm Burns & McDonnell.

1917

Oldest Continuously Operating Jazz Club in the US

Mutual Musicians Foundation

1823 Highland Ave., Kansas City, MO

Step inside the unassuming building just off 18th and Vine's main thoroughfare and you're instantly part of music history.

Built in 1904, the Mutual Musicians Foundation started as a six-unit apartment building before it was purchased in 1917 by Musicians Local 627, also known as the Colored Musicians Union. Any black musician playing jazz in Kansas City—regardless of their hometown or fame—had to register with Local 627 to get paid or file a grievance. That made the Foundation not just office space but a bustling event venue whose stage played host to renowned musicians like Charlie "Bird" Parker, Count Basie, and Ella Fitzgerald.

Many performers would book gigs at other venues around Kansas City and wouldn't necessarily only appear at the Mutual Musicians Foundation. Instead, the venue become a rollicking after-hours spot where musicians would gather postshow for jam sessions lasting into the wee hours to experiment with songs and techniques. This free-form expression helped cultivate Kansas City jazz, "influenced by New Orleans Jazz and ragtime creating a hard-swinging, blues-based musical style," as written by the University of Central Missouri's Stuart Hoy and Glyne Gee for Historic Missouri.

You can still catch all-night jam sessions on Friday and Saturday nights, when doors open at 1:30 a.m. and musicians might play until dawn. Consider a late afternoon or early evening coffee (or a nap) so you can stay awake for the fun.

"Painted music notes dance along the exterior of the building, and a plaque next to the front door touts its status as a National Historic Landmark in 1981," wrote Virginia Brown for Atlas Obscura. "Inside, over a hundred years of cigarette smoke and sweat are embedded in the wood-paneled walls." That image gives new meaning to the phrase "If these walls could talk," right?

Local 627 merged with another union, Local 34, in 1970, bringing an end to the union but not to the Foundation. The jams continue, and the Mutual Musicians Foundation is the only venue in Missouri with a liquor permit that allows drink sales until 6 a.m.

Take the sounds of the Mutual Musicians Foundation with you wherever you go. The Foundation's companion radio station, KOJH-LP 100.5 FM, streams online at KOJHFM.org.

Live jazz beckons from the heart of Kansas City's 18th and Vine District.

1991

Oldest (and Only) Negro Leagues Baseball Museum

Negro Leagues Baseball Museum

1616 E 18th St., Kansas City, MO

You also read in this book that a former YMCA building in Kansas City's 18th and Vine neighborhood hosted the meetings that formed the Negro National League in 1920. Down the street from this landmark building is another must-visit, especially for baseball fans. The Negro Leagues Baseball Museum opened in a one-room office in 1991—not much space for exhibits, right?

A hardworking group of board members led by chairman John "Buck" O'Neil undertook fundraising and other work to move the museum into its current 10,000-square-foot home, where it shares space with the American Jazz Museum as part of the cultural complex, the Museums at 18th and Vine.

A tour through the Negro Leagues Baseball Museum is simultaneously energizing and sobering. Consider this quote published in an 1885 *Sporting Life* article about Bud Fowler, widely believed to be the first black man to play professional baseball, displayed beneath Fowler's protective gear.

"Fowler, the crack colored second baseman, is still in Denver, Colorado, disengaged. The poor fellow's skin is against him. With his splendid abilities he would long ago have been on some good club had his color been white instead of black. Those who know say there is no better second baseman in the country; he

The Coors Field of Legends immortalizes 10 Negro Leagues players, and you can run the bases with them.

is besides a good batter and fine base-runner."

Fowler continued to have a truly trailblazing and remarkable career—and that energy infuses every exhibit throughout the museum. Learn more about the women of the Negro Leagues, see original uniforms and marvel at beautifully preserved dresswear. The Kansas City Monarchs were so beloved throughout the city that black churches would adjust Sunday service times to accommodate baseball games. Baseball fans would head to the ballpark straight from church, "dressed to the nines." That tradition continues today as part of the Kansas City Royals' "Salute to the Negro Leagues" annual celebration.

Your path through the museum will lead to a truly exhilarating display: the Coors Field of Legends, a mock baseball diamond complete with bronze sculptures of 10 legendary Negro Leagues players, positioned as if they're mid-game. You can step onto the field and even run the bases, so be sure you're wearing appropriate shoes!

Each February in recognition of black History Month, the Kansas City Royals and the Royals Foundation provide funding so that visitors can explore the museum free of charge.

1863

OLDEST BLACK CHURCH

SECOND BAPTIST CHURCH

3620 E 39th St., Kansas City, MO

A disclaimer: This is a tricky designation because of the number of religious denominations that exist in Kansas City. Yet in the true spirit of this book series, the search focused on identifying the true oldest black church in the city.

Second Baptist Church of Kansas City and its sister church, Allen Chapel AME, are the dual homes of "the oldest black congregation in the city," according to a commemorative article produced by the Second Baptist Church.

Upon the issuance of the Emancipation Proclamation, people formerly classified as slaves traveled up the Mississippi and Missouri Rivers, hoping to find safety and prosperity in the Kansas City area (especially Kansas).

Population numbers swelled along the Missouri River in a community called Missouri City, home to employees of the Armour Packing House. Reverand Clark Moore began gathering worshippers on those same river banks (today, the intersection of 4th Street and Troost Avenue) in a group he called "Straggler's Camp."

The group continued to grow, and in late 1863 Rev. Moore (assisted by a second reverend) gave members a choice in formalizing their denominational affiliation. Two-thirds of the group chose Baptist; the other third chose Methodist, resulting in the eventual construction of Second Baptist Church of Kansas City and Allen Chapel AME.

Second Baptist's first physical location was built at 10th and Charlotte Streets in 1898, opening just in time to host that year's National Baptist Convention. In the 1920s, congregants

Courtesy of the Historic Marker Database

temporarily met at the Paseo YMCA (birthplace of the Negro Baseball League) until fire damage at the church could be repaired. The church would relocate again before arriving at its current home at 39th and Monroe Streets in 1963.

A fun fact? During a segment on KCUR's *Up to Date* to recognize Second Baptist's 150-year anniversary in 2013, writer Stephen Steigman and host Steve Kraske noted that "the church has been led by just eight head preachers," an impressive collection of tenure! Additionally, current pastor Rev. Dr. Vernon Howard is a graduate of William Jewell College.

Other historically significant black churches in the area include St. Monica Catholic Church in 18th and Vine, the city's first black Catholic church; St. James AME and First Baptist, one of two oldest black congregations in Kansas City, Kansas, dating back to 1859; and the Northland's White Oak Chapel, the only surviving example of the black community called White Oak. The church was moved to its current location, 5410 NE Oak Ridge Dr., and restored by local organization Friends of Sacred Structures (FOSSKC.org).

1807–1885

Oldest Time Period Represented by a Living History Museum

Shoal Creek Living History Museum

7000 NE Barry Rd., Kansas City, MO

Welcome to a slice of 19th-century life! The Kansas City area is home to numerous living history museums (and they're all worth a visit!), but Shoal Creek represents the furthest jump back in time, giving visitors a glimpse of life just as the 19th century began.

Shoal Creek is the name of a mixed-use Northland community that includes homes and apartments, businesses, Shoal Creek Golf Course, and attractions like the Shoal Creek Living History Museum.

The museum grounds represent what was previously known as Heritage Village, one of many frontier communities that emerged as riverfront development expanded throughout Clay and Platte Counties.

"Being on the major trade route between Liberty Landing and Barry and the Oregon Trail, Heritage Village was fueled by trade and the outfitting of travelers moving on into Oregon," according to historic documents provided by the museum. "Trappers, farmers, blacksmiths, the grocer—all were an integral part of the roots of Heritage Village."

And it's that vibrant microcosm that you can explore today on a sprawling property that includes a reproduction of a grist mill, a variety of homes, an 1884 Baptist church, Missouri

Left: Shoal Creek reenactors. Right: Shoal Creek Trenton Mansion
Photos courtesy of the Shoal Creek Living History Museum

City's original 1868 city hall and jail, a school—and that's just the start. Altogether, the museum includes 13 historic buildings, many of which were relocated from different areas in Kansas City's Northland to provide a more comprehensive picture of 19th-century life throughout the area, both close to the river and further inland.

The museum is also home to a bison herd, which you may see during your visit. American Bison—the largest surviving mammal in North America—were especially abundant before European settlement until excessive hunting vastly reduced the bison's population, especially in Missouri.

Like most museums, the Shoal Creek Living History Museum maintains an active events calendar. For a deeper dive into a particular year, consider visiting during the Pioneer Days series, held one Saturday a month from June through September. Details: shoalcreeklivinghistorymuseum.com.

1903

OLDEST FINE-DINING RESTAURANT

THE SAVOY

219 W 9th St., Kansas City, MO

Construction on the Savoy Hotel began in 1888, creating the first major hotel en route from Union Depot in the West Bottoms (home to the stockyards and Livestock Exchange) into Kansas City's bustling downtown. A building expansion added the Savoy Grill in 1903, a luxurious space enveloped in dark oak with terrazzo floors and several murals by Edward Holslag, all designed in a blend of Neoclassic and Art Nouveau.

Towering booth seats framed by dark green brick walls provide a sort of intimate seclusion that befits a business meeting or a romantic night out. Harry Truman had a favorite booth—number 4—that's still marked with a discreet plaque.

When the Savoy Grill first opened, only men could eat or drink there. Women were relegated to a separate dining room. The restaurant also flouted Prohibition, maintaining liquor sales under the protection of "Boss" Tom Pendergast.

The original Savoy Grill suffered extensive fire damage in 2014, yet the structure and a number of interior elements were saved. The restaurant reopened as the Savoy in 2018, part of 21c Museum Hotel's acquisition of both the hotel and restaurant.

It's estimated that 80 percent of the Savoy's current interior is original, including the stained-glass windows and much of the oak work. Holslag's murals are preserved and protected with the help of official designation from the Smithsonian. And if you look closely toward the top of the restaurant's lengthy bar, you might notice hand-painted scarab adornments. They were discovered while repairing smoke damage from the earlier fire.

A menu of contemporary American cuisine is the perfect complement to the historic surroundings, offering a range of seafood, grilled meat, and pasta. Brunch is delicious yet underrated, and the cocktail menu is a nod to Kansas City's spirited history, a mix of classics like the 1880-era old-fashioned and modern twists including the 2024-created cassowary with amaro, mezcal, blueberry pineapple, and coffee. You'll also find a Tiki classic, the Jungle Bird, on the menu—it's been a popular go-to for Kansas Citians since its creation in the late 1970s.

As of this writing, the Savoy (hotel and restaurant) have changed ownership from 21c Museum Hotels to Hilton, becoming part of the Tapestry Collection. Another historic property, the Oread in Lawrence, is part of the same portfolio.

1927–1929

Oldest Local Apartment Buildings Designed by a Woman

Nelle Peters, Architect, The Literary Apartments

4800 and 4804 Jefferson St., Kansas City, MO

Courtesy of KCPL

"By the time architect Nelle Peters (1884–1974) had retired in 1967 at the age of 83, almost every neighborhood and area in Kansas City, Missouri, had been enhanced by her architectural designs," wrote Sherry Piland for Missouri State University.

The North Dakota native attended Buena Vista College in Storm Lake, Iowa, as a preparatory and collegiate student. She didn't want to take business courses; instead, at the urging of her sister, she moved to Sioux City to channel her love of art and math into architecture.

Peters joined a small architecture firm as a "draftslady" in 1903, then relocated to Kansas City to help open a branch of the Iowa firm. She deepened her architectural knowledge through correspondence courses; then, in 1909, she left the firm and struck out on her own.

"Although her business grew slowly, she soon found a niche by specializing in the design of apartment buildings and hotels," Piland wrote. In the 1920s, Peters also expanded her portfolio to include commercial buildings, starting with an addition to Southside Hospital and the McConahay Building, site of Walt Disney's Laugh-O-Gram Studios.

Peters's work designing apartment buildings noticeably increased as she began working with builder and developer Charles E. Phillips, president of Phillips Building Company. Her projects for Phillips included a series of apartment buildings along the western edge of Country Club Plaza known as "The Literary Block," each building named for a famous writer including Mark Twain, Robert Louis Stevenson, and Robert Browning. The apartments remain inhabited today, the stylistic brick and stone facades providing eye-catching streetscapes in an area densely populated with residential and commercial buildings. Additional locations of the apartments include 4746 and 4809 Roanoke Parkway and 700, 708, 712, 720, and 804 West 48th Street.

Left: Literary Apartment at 48th and Jefferson Streets. Right: The Robert Louis Stevenson building, part of the Literary Apartments

Among other significant projects in Peters's prolific portfolio: downtown Kansas City's Ambassador Hotel (the largest hotel built in Kansas City at that time), a lavish Italianate mansion for Phillips, and the Madrid and Granada apartments. Peters also designed buildings in other cities, including Wichita's Commodore Hotel and Topeka's Senate Apartments.

Other notable Kansas City women in architecture include Mary Rockwell Hook, creator of the first architectural design in Kansas City to include a swimming pool; Alice Jackson, who created around 20 local homes mostly south of the Plaza; and Mary Colter, designer of the Fred Harvey Restaurants, including the original location inside Union Station.

1989/1884

Oldest Continuously Operating Brewery

Boulevard Brewing Company

2501 Southwest Blvd., Kansas City, MO

Free State Brewery

636 Massachusetts St., Lawrence, KS

Heim Brewing

2700 Guinotte Ave., Kansas City, MO

In the early 20th century, one stretch of Kansas City near State Line Road in the West Bottoms was so packed with saloons it became known as "the wettest block in the world."

That reputation continues today. The Kansas City metro is home to approximately 50 breweries, many of which have roots in the mid-19th century. That scourge Prohibition, however, at least temporarily shuttered all local commercial breweries, so in terms of identifying Kansas City's oldest continuously operating brewery, the field narrows—as does the applicable time frame.

Research shows 1989 as a pivotal year for local breweries. In nearby Lawrence, Kansas, Free State Brewery became the first brewery to operate in Kansas since Prohibition. And in Kansas City, a local legacy was born when Boulevard Brewing Company opened with its first signature brew, Boulevard Pale Ale. Boulevard is now the largest specialty brewer in the Midwest.

John McDonald, the brains behind Boulevard, had dabbled in home brewing after an inspiring trip to Europe gave him a

The Tours and Rec Building is a newer addition to the Boulevard Brewing Company infrastructure. Courtesy of Visit KC

chance to dig into European brewing history. As his knowledge grew, so did his dreams: He wanted to open a craft brewery in Kansas City.

"I want to do something different," he said in an article on Boulevard's website. "'I want to make big beers, a variety of beers, beers with color and flavor and aroma and body, beers for real beer lovers.'"

And he did just that. Boulevard has expanded into a wide array of beers and, in recent years, added canned cocktails, fruit- and herb-flavored seltzers, and three nonalcoholic options. Belgium-based Duvel Moortgart bought Boulevard in 2013, but the brewery and a multistory tours and recreation complex remain in Kansas City.

Going solely by date in operation, Heim Brewing is likely the first brewery that started in Kansas City, opening in 1884 as the Bavarian Brewing Company. The name would soon change to Heim Brewing when the company moved into a former sugar refinery in the East Bottoms neighborhood and became a significant presence in the community, investing in the Kansas City Cowboys professional baseball team (kicked out of the National League one year later for rowdiness) and, in 1900, opening Electric Park, an amusement park inspired by Coney Island.

The brewery ended operations during Prohibition, but in recent years, a new chapter of the Heim Brewing legacy is underway. In 2018, local distillery J. Rieger & Co. converted the former East Bottoms bottling plant to its new distillery, including a small-scale Electric Park. At the request of the J. Rieger team, KC Bier Co. began brewing lager-style Heim Bier, served on tap at the distillery and available in restaurants and retail locations throughout the city. Maybe the world's wettest block will make a triumphant comeback, too!

To keep tabs (pun intended) on Kansas City's beer history author Pete Dulin is a knowledgeable source. He's written three books on the subject, exploring brewing history in Kansas City as well as the city's two home states.

1985

OLDEST LGBTQ BAR

SIDEKICKS

3707 Main St., Kansas City, MO

A census of past and current LGBTQ bars written and published by David Jackson in 2016 as part of the Gay and Lesbian Archive of Mid-America brings mixed emotions upon perusal. A large number of LGBTQ hangouts, especially from the 1970s and '80s, are no longer open, creating a diminished nightlife scene that a variety of LGBTQ business leaders and advocates are working to expand.

In fact, several new LGBTQ nightlife spots have opened in the last three years; but here we're focused on those that came first. Although it has operated under three different names, Sidekicks Saloon is the city's longest-running LGBTQ bar, first opening its doors in 1981 as Open Range. Four years later the property morphed into the second incarnation of Connections Lounge, which had originally opened in 1979. Then, in 1985, the Midtown hangout became Sidekicks Saloon, a country-and-western bar.

Prolific drag performer and businessperson Robert "Buddy" Taylor bought Sidekicks in the summer of 2021. The bar maintains its saloon-esque roots, but has also expanded to include drag shows, Latin-themed nights, and karaoke.

"The fact is that Sidekicks Saloon may have closed if Buddy had not bought it," wrote Paul Proffett for OUTvoices. "And the upgrades he's made are impressive—new bar tops, tiling, improved restrooms and nifty freeway shield and neon sign designs give the place a clean and expansive feel that still preserves the country and western look."

Among the most impressive things about Sidekicks—aside from its tenure—are its operating hours. The bar is open until 3 a.m. seven days a week, so make plans to grab a drink whenever your travels bring you to Kansas City. The bar doesn't accept credits cards, so bring cash or hit up the on-site ATM.

Make time for Joel Barrett's Rainbow Tour while you explore. The VoiceMap-guided driving tour winds you on a fascinating path from the University of Missouri–Kansas City to the Museum of Kansas City, highlighting key places and moments in Kansas City LGBTQ history as you go. One example: Womontown, a 1980s neighborhood started by Drea Nedelsky and her girlfriend, Maryann Hopper, to create a community "where they could be themselves without fear, a place where women could walk hand-in-hand down the street without the judgements and criticisms normally encountered in the 'straight world,'" according to a documentary produced by KCPT. Take the tour at kcrainbowtour.com.

Courtesy of Do816

ca. 1840

OLDEST AREA CEMETERY

BARRY COMMUNITY CEMETERY

1317 NW Barry Rd., Kansas City, MO

Forgive the wording, but . . . here lies another local historic debate. With an explosion in population inevitably comes a rapid growth in local cemeteries, and the early days of Kansas City were no exception.

While large public cemeteries like Union Hill Cemetery (developed in 1857) and Forest Hill Calvary Cemetery (developed in 1888) tend to draw consistent attention, there are an untold number of small cemeteries scattered throughout the metro area, making it more complex to determine the actual oldest.

Among these is Barry Community Cemetery. Barry was founded in the 1820s as "an unincorporated community in Kansas City North straddling the Clay County–Platte County line northeast of Gladstone," according to *Kansas City: A Place in Time*. "The town began as a trading post for Sac and Fox Indians and was named for William Taylor Barry, appointed postmaster general under President Andrew Jackson."

Barry's post office proved to be a hot spot, as it was the only stagecoach stop along an approximately 50-mile route from Liberty Landing in Missouri to Fort Leavenworth in Kansas.

The small cemetery is home to several graves, mostly from the

1830s. The earliest legible date, as noted in *Kansas City: A Place in Time*, is 1815.

History enthusiasts would do well to also stop at Union Hill Cemetery, the oldest public cemetery in Kansas City, Missouri, and the resting place of more than 55,000 souls, including artist George Caleb Bingham, Westport founder John Calvin McCoy, Hattie Drisdom Kearney (the first Black person to be buried in the cemetery), and Tillman Crabtree, Kansas City's first policeman.

Another notable but often unnoticed cemetery isn't far from Barry. Gash Cemetery (398 NW Barry Rd.) is the final resting place for early residents of Gashland, a produce farming and marketing community developed by Joseph Gash. Productive orchards, berry fields, and vineyards kept the community prosperous, and it still exists today as the Gashland/Nashua neighborhood. Gravestones in Gash Cemetery date back to the late 1830s.

The two Northland cemeteries mentioned—Barry Community and Gash—are separated by a mere three-minute drive along Barry Road, one of the major commercial thoroughfares north of the river. These historic graves are now adjacent to big-box retail stores, a stark contrast that exists in so many cities around the world as past meets present.

1887

OLDEST LOCAL DISTILLERY

J. RIEGER & CO.

2700 Guinotte Ave., Kansas City, MO

What pairs perfectly with a steak dinner? A fine whiskey, of course—and so Austrian immigrant Jacob Rieger opened Jacob Rieger & Company, a whiskey-focused business, in 1887 in the West Bottoms District near the Livestock Exchange.

Like enterprising cobbler C.H. Hyer, Rieger quickly spotted a need for a mail-order business and grew to be "the largest mail-order whiskey purveyor in the world," according to the distillery, shipping more than 100 alcoholic products to a customer list 250,000 strong.

Prohibition closed Rieger's doors, and the brand was precariously close to being forever lost in time—until Rieger's great-great-great-grandson, Andy, stepped in.

Andy's attention was piqued when his family's namesake hotel, the Rieger, reopened after a renovation in 2010. The newly revitalized building in downtown Kansas City's Crossroads Arts District was home to a main-floor fine dining restaurant and—down a precariously steep flight of stairs—Manifesto, a speakeasy founded by Ryan Maybee as a nod to the dimly lit hideaways of Kansas City's past.

Andy and Ryan met, and Ryan suggested restarting the Rieger family's whiskey brand as part of the bar's menu. Andy moved to Kansas City from Dallas in 2014 to focus on building J. Rieger & Co. with Ryan. Master distiller Dave Pickerell joined the team, bringing his experience with Maker's Mark bourbon to the task of creating a fresh J. Rieger & Co. whiskey.

"We created our own style of whiskey by utilizing different whiskies distilled from different distilleries, along with sherry wine to be blended in with the whiskey," Andy wrote for Inc.com. "The addition of sherry was a practice that was very popular in the late 1800s, early 1900s. And the original J. Rieger & Co. blended sherry onsite."

J. Rieger & Co. whiskey is now available in 27 states and Washington, DC. The distillery's spirits portfolio is extensive and includes whiskey, gin, vodka, and amaro. Andy, a University of Missouri alumni, has also partnered with his alma mater and the University of Kansas to create custom-branded spirits and canned cocktails. The distillery, itself a historic brand, also perpetuates local history through specialty releases like the Fielder's Choice Collection, developed in partnership with the Negro Leagues Baseball Museum to create four whiskeys inspired by iconic Negro League teams: the Kansas City Monarchs, the Chicago American Giants, the St. Louis Stars, and the Homestead Grays.

It's easy to spend a full day at this expansive, multistory distilling facility. Take the guided tour to learn more about the distilling process, then peruse a main-floor exhibit that details J. Rieger's history. A number of spaces beckon when you're ready for a cocktail: the upstairs Monogram Lounge, an outdoor cocktail garden called Electric Park, and the Hey! Hey! Club, which simultaneously evokes the feeling of a stately home library, complete with comfortably worn leather seating, and a dim, cozy speakeasy. Give yourself a little liquid courage from a J. Rieger cocktail, then be sure to exit the distillery via the spiraling metal slide that winds from the Monogram Lounge to the main entrance area.

1910

Oldest Woman-Built Event Space

Drexel Hall

3301 Baltimore Ave., Kansas City, MO

Kansas City simply wouldn't be the same without the many brilliant, enterprising, and often overlooked women who literally helped shape the city and, in turn, also left their mark here.

One of these women was Barbara Drexel Bescher, an Austrian immigrant who arrived in Kansas City in the latter part of the 19th century. She worked with her husband, John, at the grocery store he owned at 15th and Main in the 1870s, but by 1896, the two had divorced.

Bescher didn't receive any financial support from her ex-husband and needed to care for seven children. She began operating a market stall, selling vegetables and other goods. As she became more financially stable, she looked for other opportunities to expand her business. During a drive down what's now Linwood Boulevard, Bescher noticed a lot for sale and had a good feeling about the potential development of the surrounding area. That same day, Bescher made an offer on the building; after a bit of haggling, she secured the land for $6,750.

Bescher opened Drexel Hall in 1910 as a stately, multipurpose event space—and it didn't take long for the community to keep Drexel Hall busy. School concerts, dances and balls, plays, benefits—the Drexel Hall event calendar stayed full. The building played an increasingly important role in local politics, too, hosting local suffrage association meetings and, in the 1960s, serving as the site of several political rallies and labor-movement gatherings.

Today, Drexel Hall remains a sought-after event venue, especially for weddings. The community focus continues under the leadership of the Kansas City Irish Center, which established permanent office space in Drexel Hall in 2016 (they were previously located in Union Station). Drexel Hall's location in the midst of several Irish neighborhoods and proximity to beloved landmarks like Browne's Irish Market and Our Lady of Perpetual Help (Redemptorist) Church makes it a natural gathering spot for Irish Center meetings, events, live music, and more.

For the full Drexel Hall experience, check the Kansas City Irish Center's website before your visit: www.IrishCenterKC.org. A steady stream of programming, including dance, genealogy, and crafting, is held throughout the year, and Drexel Hall gets especially busy in the weeks leading up to St. Patrick's Day and also Kansas City Irish Fest, held Labor Day weekend at downtown Kansas City's Crown Center.

1899

Oldest Continuously Operating Fountain

The Women's Leadership Fountain

9th St. and the Paseo, Kansas City, MO

You can't write about Kansas City without at least a mention of fountains—after all, Kansas City is the "City of Fountains." Fountains here number more than 200, a total second only to Rome.

Given the European influences in George Kessler and August Meyer's parks and boulevard system plan, which later launched the City Beautiful movement, it's not surprising that these early aesthetic visionaries latched on to fountains as a way to provide both beauty and function. Many of the city's first fountains were less eye-catching and had rather simple designs. Their purpose? Keeping horses hydrated. (Fun fact: the city's only still-functioning horse-trough fountain can be seen at the Wyandotte County Historical Museum, 632 North 126th Street, Bonner Springs, Kansas.)

Unfortunately, Kansas City's first fountain is no longer functioning. Its second fountain, designed by Kessler and John VanBrunt, opened in 1899 at an intersection along the Paseo, one of five boulevards created as part of the aforementioned parks and boulevards plan.

Full disclosure: The fountain did endure a significant period of disuse, likely more from neglect than any other reason. In 1970, the fountain's basin was excavated and repaired, and the fountain resumed operation. Nearly 20 years later, the Central Exchange—an organization created to help women achieve their full potential—led a fundraising effort to further restore the fountain.

Since then, the Women's Leadership Fountain stands and operates in tribute to 13 women who made significant contributions to Kansas City. They were Myrtle Page Fillmore, Phoebe Jane Ess, Alice Berry Graham, Mary Harmon Weeks, Bertha Manheimer Leiberman, Katherine Berry Richardson, Nelle Elizabeth Peters, Caroline Benton Cockfair, Ada Crogman Franklin, Guadalupe Bribiesca de Garcia, Madalyn Pinkston Brock, Ellen (Nell) Donnelly Reed, and Esther Swirk Brown.

The Women's Leadership Fountain is the oldest fountain built and still operating in Kansas City. The city's oldest existing fountain, however, resides within the Nelson-Atkins Museum of Art's Rozelle Court. The Fountain Basin dates to 220 C.E.

Kansas City celebrates Greater Kansas City Fountain Day in April, when fountains are simultaneously turned on to resume post-winter operation—a sure sign that spring is here! If you notice fountain waters dyed unexpected colors during your visit, it's likely in recognition of a sports-related achievement or community cause.

1911

Oldest Studio Where Walt Disney Worked

Disney's Laugh-O-Gram Studio

1127 E 31st St., Kansas City, MO

Walt Disney was one of several famous people who got his start in Kansas City. After moving here with his family from Marceline, Missouri, in 1911, Disney worked as a commercial artist for a local advertising company and, during his off hours, would gather with friends or work solo to create cartoons that became Disney's first animated films in 1920.

Disney founded his first professional film studio in a Nelle Peters–designed building in Kansas City's Midtown. At one point, Laugh-O-Gram Studio employed 11 people and served as both Disney's office and home when he could no longer afford rent.

Let's pause here to set the record straight. Yes, Mickey Mouse was created in Kansas City—but not by Disney, as untold accounts would have us believe. The famous mouse was actually the brainchild of Disney's friend and business partner, Ub Iwerks, who created the cartoon character in 1928. Jeff Ryan, author of *A Mouse Divided: How Ub Iwerks Became Forgotten, and Walt Disney Became Uncle Walt*, explained in an episode of KCUR's *A People's History of Kansas City* podcast that "Mickey is basically the child of two dads."

That said, Disney still played an integral role in the development of Mickey Mouse as a staple of animation and pop culture. Disney developed Mickey's personality and also voiced the character for years.

Current exterior of Laugh-O-Gram Studio

The building that housed Laugh-O-Gram Studio remains, but it is in need of renovation and repair. A group of Kansas City developers and advocates led by Butch Rigby, owner of Screenland Theater and a longtime developer, launched the Thank you, Walt Disney, Inc. initiative and campaign, which has several goals. Plans call for the complete renovation of the Laugh-O-Gram building, adding a state-of-the-art teaching facility, a theater, and lecture hall in addition to exhibits and re-created office space that pay homage to Disney and his team of animators.

Stay up-to-date with the Thank You, Walt Disney effort at www.ThankYouWaltDisney.org. During your visit, download the Clio app and take the Walt Disney's Kansas City tour, a self-guided driving route that encompasses 13 notable Kansas City locations in Disney's life and career.

1909

OLDEST GLASS CURTAIN WALL ARCHITECTURE

BOLEY CLOTHING COMPANY BUILDING

1130 Walnut St., Kansas City, MO

Meet Canada-born Louis S. Curtiss, an architect who immigrated to Kansas City in 1887 and later became known as "the Frank Lloyd Wright of Kansas City."

Many Curtiss-designed buildings and homes still stand in Kansas City today, including the Boley Clothing Company Building, built in 1909. The six-story building was among the first in the world to use glass curtain walls, specifically steel with glass construction (a departure from earlier buildings made primarily of brick or stone).

"When first completed, the building was considered stark and even ugly in comparison to the ornamented style common during that time period," wrote Jim Richards.

File this under "don't judge a book by its cover"; the structural design created to support such an exterior was wildly complex. More than 15,000 square feet of glass were used to create the visual effect that the glass wall envelops the building. Curtiss would continue embracing the concept of a glass curtain wall, incorporating this exterior aesthetic into his own mixed-use building at 1120 McGee Street that included main-level studio space and luxurious second-floor living quarters complete with a rooftop courtyard.

As Kansas City–based publisher Andrews McMeel Universal prepared to relocate downtown from its Country Club Plaza office in the early 2000s, they worked with local companies Helix Architecture + Design Inc. and McCown Gordon

Construction to revive the multi-floor space as Andrews McMeel's new headquarters. Several sections of the building were in disrepair, yet Andrews McMeel leadership emphasized restoration to protect the Boley Building's architectural and historic significance. That included preservation of the glass curtain wall, considered too stark for its era but now reflecting (pun intended) a flair for modernity that was decades ahead of its time.

Andrews McMeel Universal employees have been known to adorn several of the street-facing windows with Post-it notes art inspired by several of AMU's iconic comics properties, including The Far Side, Calvin and Hobbes, Doonesbury, Ziggy, *and* Cathy.

Courtesy of KCPL

1855

OLDEST BRICK HOUSE

HARRIS-KEARNEY HOUSE

4000 Baltimore Ave., Kansas City, MO

The changing ownership of the Harris-Kearney House is an apt microcosm of the pro- and antislavery fight that raged within Kansas City, especially across the state line.

John Harris, one of the people credited with helping to develop Westport, opened the well-known Harris Hotel in 1845. It became a popular stop for people headed west. The Harris family home, a two-story brick antebellum Greek Revival house, was completed in 1855 with at least some of the labor provided by the enslaved people owned by Harris. Later, during the Civil War, both the Harris Hotel and the home would be occupied by Union soldiers.

After Harris passed in 1873, Irish immigrant Charles Kearney inherited the home (he had previously married John's daughter, Josephine) and continued working to build Kansas City into a booming commercial hub, especially after the construction of the Hannibal Bridge to ferry railroad traffic across the Missouri River.

Historical accounts indicate that the Kearney family did not own slaves, with one critical exception. Kearney purchased 11-year-old Harriet "Hattie" Drisdom Kearney in 1855 to keep her close to family members who were enslaved by the family of Henrietta

Harris, John's wife. Two years later, Kearney gave Hattie her freedom. Yet prior to the Civil War—and, more importantly, the Emancipation Proclamation—Hattie found limited options for supporting herself and instead opted to stay with the Kearney family, working as a housekeeper. Upon her death in 1927, Hattie became the first black person to be buried in the "Whites Only" section of Kansas City's Union Hill Cemetery.

The Harris-Kearney House, relocated from its original location at Westport Road and Main Street in 1922, remains open as office space of the Westport Historical Society. The house closed in 2022 for a combination of historic restoration and modern enhancements and reopened to tours in summer 2024. Now, visitors can explore various rooms in the house that feature displays detailing 19th-century life. Don't miss exterior displays, too, including the front wagon wheels and axle from an 1860s Conestoga Wagon that originally stood outside Westport Shopping Center for more than six decades.

Once inside the home, imagine standing or sitting at the windows and watching the Battle of Westport unfold. That's what the Harris grandchildren did in October 1864.

1927

Oldest Existing Ballroom

El Torreon Ballroom

3101 Gillham Plaza, Kansas City, MO

Jazz isn't the only type of music to captivate Kansas City. The early 20th century saw a citywide love of big band and orchestra performances, creating the need for performance spaces that could also accommodate dancing—ballrooms.

Among the earliest of such establishments in Kansas City was El Torreon, which opened in 1927 as a two-room ballroom—plenty of space to spread out and dance, provided you were white.

El Torreon shuttered in 1934 as a result of the Great Depression, but the Midtown building stayed true to its entertainment roots. The building became a supper club and later a roller-skating rink as the recreational pastime exploded in popularity in the late 1930s.

Live music returned to the former El Torreon in the 1970s as the Cowtown Ballroom. And although the Cowtown didn't last long (it was open only three years), the venue hosted some of music's biggest names, cementing Kansas City as a not-to-be-missed live music destination. Van Morrison, Linda Ronstadt, Alice Cooper, and Frank Zappa were among the performers to take the stage at the Cowtown Ballroom, a venue that also became a refuge for Kansas City's counterculture amid anti-war protests, civil rights demonstrations, and the feminist movement.

More recently, El Torreon opened its doors in the early 2000s to hardcore, metal, punk, and ska performers in a smaller front space dubbed the "El Torreon Concert Room." Other parts of the space—including the upper and lower ballrooms and concert space—have been revitalized and host a variety of events ranging from weddings and art shows to concerts and business meetings. A little less punk rock, to be sure, but more important that the legacy continues for newer generations of Kansas Citians who crave the performance, spectacle, and community that were hallmarks of the ballroom dancing craze, which grew past upper-class gatekeeping and gained mainstream appeal in the early 1900s.

Visit the Museum of Kansas City (3218 Gladstone Blvd.) to see an in-depth exhibit on El Torreon. Snap a selfie in front of a giant mirror ball (or disco ball) that used to slowly spin over El Torreon's dance floor.

1875

OLDEST SYNAGOGUE

THE TEMPLE, CONGREGATION B'NAI JEHUDAH

1515 E Linwood Blvd., Kansas City, MO

As Kansas City settlement continued into the late 19th century, a group of families gathered to form the Temple, Congregation B'nai Jehudah, one of the nation's oldest Reform Jewish Congregations.

The congregation first met in Elmwood Cemetery (the resting place of prominent Kansas Citians like Kersey Coates, Mattie Rhodes, and the city's first mayor, William Gregory) before building a permanent sanctuary at 6th and Wyandotte Streets in 1875. The expanding congregation needed a larger gathering place just 10 years later, so a new temple was built in 1885 at the southwest corner of 11th and Oak Streets. (Note: Part of the temple's foundation still stands today.)

Courtesy of Synagogues of the South

The ever-growing congregation moved to a third temple at 1515 East Linwood Boulevard, a structure designed by architecture firm Howe, Hult & Cutler and built by Taylor & Winn in 1908. Notable features of the stately building include six fluted Doric columns along the front entrance topped by hand-cut stone lettering that reads, "My House Shall Be a House of Prayer for All Peoples."

Two senior rabbis served at the Linwood temple, including Samuel S. Mayerberg, who launched a vocal fight against the corrupt machine rule that dominated Kansas City's politics through the first part of the 20th century. Despite harassment and threats, Rabbi Mayerberg stayed focused on his work and would emerge victorious as the city's political machine collapsed in 1939 after Tom Pendergast was arrested, tried, convicted, and sent to the Leavenworth Federal Penitentiary for tax fraud.

The congregation would move again to 69th Street and Holmes before settling into its current home at 12320 Nall Avenue in Overland Park. The state-of-the-art facility includes a 300-seat chapel, library, and social hall.

As for the Linwood temple, it remains standing but is currently unoccupied, and much of the property is fenced off.

A number of resources are available to learn more about the history of Kansas City's Jewish community. Download the Clio app to follow the Kansas City Jewish Heritage Trail, a driving or biking tour. Or explore articles, manuscripts, newspapers, and photographs collected at the Jewish Community Archives of Kansas City, part of the State Historical Society of Missouri. Find details at shsmo.org.

1907

Oldest Continuously Operating Men's Clothier

Michael's Clothing

1830 Main St., Kansas City, MO

As the KC Streetcar moves north or south along Main Street and passes Michael's Clothing near the intersection of 19th Street, the resulting snapshot shows Kansas City's past and present. It's at this busy corner that Russian immigrant Michael H. Novorr opened a combination pawn shop and men's clothing store in 1907.

Novorr eventually expanded the clothing business, eliminating the pawn store to focus on keeping Kansas City men outfitted in the finest professional and leisure attire. Michael's became family run in the 1940s when Michael's two sons, Howard and Eugene, joined their father in the retail industry. Consistently brisk business prompted the trio to expand the store in 1965, doubling the available floor space.

Eugene's son, Keith, became the third-generation owner of Michael's Clothing in 1978 and, in 2005, Keith's son, Michael, joined the family business. A trip to Michael's is worthwhile not just for the personalized shopping experience, but also for the incredible array of photos and memorabilia that line the walls. A number of Kansas City Chiefs players have made Michael's their style go-to, as have famous visitors to Kansas City like former professional wrestler Ric Flair, who frequently boasted about his impressive collection of suits, all purchased at Michael's, and Azie Taylor Morton, former US treasurer, who stopped in to shop for her husband.

It's remarkable for a business to surpass the 100-year milestone, but especially notable for a local retail store that withstood not only decades of economic and political turmoil but also the rise (and, to an extent, fall) of suburbia-focused shopping malls. Through it all, Michael's keeps customers dressed for any occasion.

Michael's Clothing is located near the KC Streetcar's Crossroads stop at 19th and Main, making a shopping trip the ideal addition to a downtown-focused day out. Michael's home neighborhood, the Crossroads Arts District, is home to an eclectic mix of galleries, boutiques, restaurants, bars, and a beloved tradition: the monthly First Fridays gallery walk.

1926

OLDEST WORLD WAR I MEMORIAL IN THE US

LIBERTY MEMORIAL (PART OF THE NATIONAL WORLD WAR I MUSEUM AND MEMORIAL)

2 Memorial Dr., Kansas City, MO

With countless cities across the US suffering casualties and other permanent effects of World War I, how did the country's only World War I memorial end up in Kansas City?

Anecdotal evidence shared by some of the museum's dedicated volunteers said Kansas Citians were especially motivated to memorialize the Great War because, per capita, Kansas City had among the highest rates of war-related casualties.

Soon after the war ended, city leaders formed the Liberty Memorial Association to create a lasting monument to those who had fought in the war. In 1919, the LMA and eager Kansas Citians raised more than $2.5 million in a mere 10 days—"the equivalent of more than $40 million today," according to the museum's website, a "staggering accomplishment [that] reflected the passion of public sentiment for the Great War that dramatically changed the world."

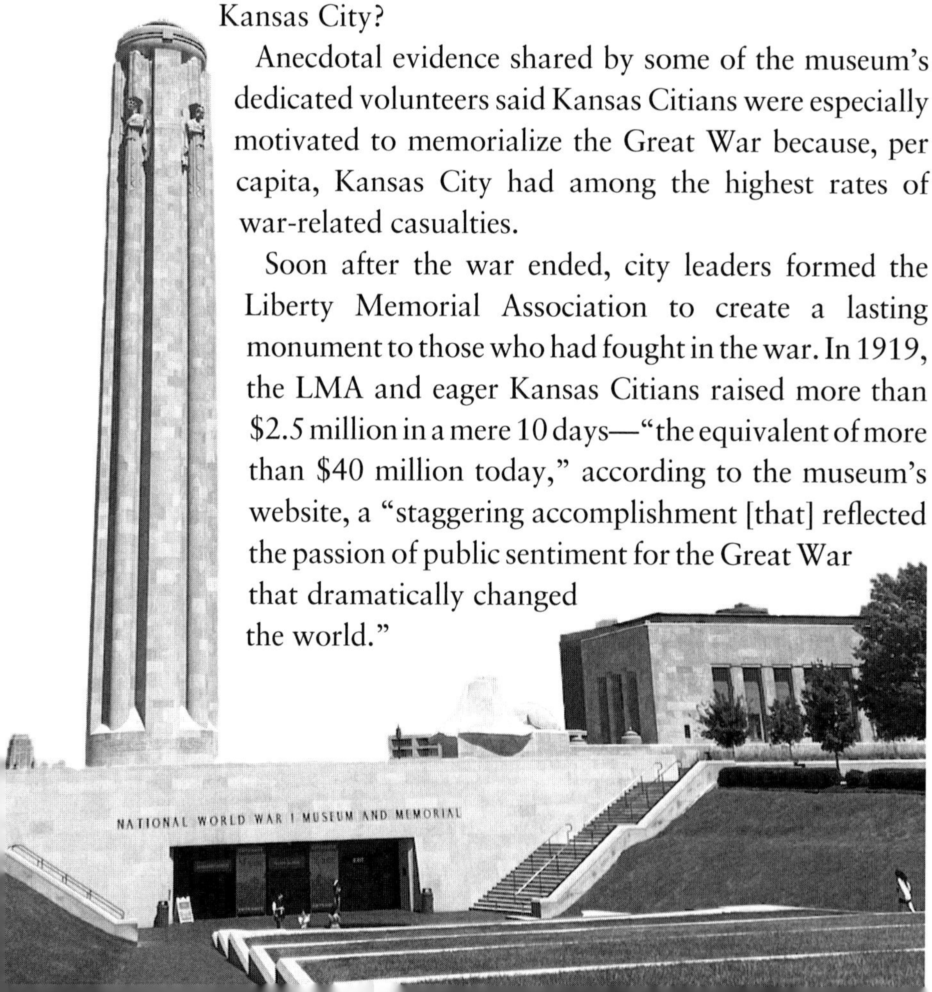

New York–based architect H. Van Buren McGonigle won a national architecture competition to design the memorial in the early 1920s, and in 1921, all five supreme Allied commanders gathered in Kansas City to dedicate the site of the Liberty Memorial.

Construction finished on McGonigle's Egyptian Revival–inspired design in 1926. The memorial includes a number of architecturally significant features that reflect the gravity and enduring impact of the memorial's inciting event. Look for two Assyrian sphinxes that guard the memorial's south entrance. As a museum summary explains, "'Memory' faces east toward the battlefields of France, shielding its eyes from the horrors of war. 'Future' faces west, shielding its eyes from an unknown future."

Additional notable design elements include four Guardian Spirits, each 40 feet tall and carved by Robert Aitken. These protectors of peace are in place to watch over the memorial from atop the 217-foot tower. Two empty cinerary urns are positioned outside of the Memory and Exhibit Halls. Carved bands of laurel encircle both urns and feature emblems of the branches of service that contributed to victory: the Army, the Navy, the Red Cross, Agriculture and Manufacturing, and Transportation.

For the full National World War I Museum and Memorial experience, purchase a combination ticket that grants access to the museum and to the top of Liberty Memorial. Quarters at the top of the memorial are tight, but docents carefully monitor visitor numbers as groups cycle in and out of the tower. Have your camera ready—once you emerge into the open air 268 feet above the museum's North Lawn, you'll be treated to some of the best views in Kansas City

---

ca. 1920s

OLDEST MIDWESTERN FILM WALK OF FAME

WALK OF FAME/FILM ROW

18th St. between Wyandotte and Central Sts., Kansas City, MO

Kansas City's location in the heart of the US not only helped make it a booming river and railroad hub; it also meant that the city was perfectly placed for all sorts of distribution, from illegitimate (Mafia-managed financial pipelines from KC to Las Vegas) to above-board, including a four-decade span as a leading film distributor for Hollywood's biggest studios like MGM, Warner Brothers, Paramount, Universal, Disney, United Artists, and others, according to Visit KC.

Film distributor offices lined several blocks along a stretch of downtown road called Film Row. The area also included film storage facilities to keep pace with the demand for easily accessible space. As Clarence Denis wrote for Flatland KC, around 800 films were produced in the US each year during the 1920s movie boom. Multiply that number by six to 10 reels of film per movie, and it's no wonder centrally located warehouse space proved a significant advantage.

As Denis described for Flatland KC, early films were created from highly flammable nitro cellulose reels, creating a pervasive threat of fire. Denis quoted Dr. Derek Long, assistant professor of media and film studies at the University of Illinois, as follows: "Basically, the local exchange areas passed municipal laws saying that all film distribution has to happen in these film rows where there are controlled laws, laws about how you build the building, how you fireproof it, all that stuff."

This view of Kansas City's Film Row dates to the mid-1940s. Courtesy of KCPL

Film Row is now part of the Crossroads Arts District, a lively, creative hub that hosts a recurring art and gallery walk on the first Friday of every month.

In addition to noting the historic plaques that designate Film Row buildings, take some time to explore Kansas City's Walk of Fame. Sidewalk stars—just like those in Hollywood—pay homage to Kansas City–born celebrities. Some of the names you'll spot? Joan Crawford, Walt Disney, Jean Harlow, and Ginger Rogers, among others. Perhaps the Walk of Fame will, at some point, be extended to include more recent Kansas City celebrities like *Saturday Night Live*'s Heidi Gardner, *Ted Lasso*'s Jason Sudeikis, and Oscar-nominated Don Cheadle.

Download the Clio app, developed by University of Missouri–Kansas City history professor David Trowbridge, to cue up the Film Row walking tour as you explore.

1982

Oldest and Largest Collection of Fine-Scale Miniatures

National Museum of Toys and Miniatures

5235 Oak St., Kansas City, MO

Let's help you get your bearings before you discover the wonders that await inside this delightful museum.

The National Museum of Toys and Miniatures opened in 1982 inside the historic Tureman Mansion, part of the University of Missouri–Kansas City campus. The stately and modern-for-its-time 1911 mansion was built by Dr. Herbert Tureman. Dr. Tureman's wife, Marie, would later lease the home to an iconic Kansas City woman: Nell Donnelly Reed, noted fashion designer and creator of the Nelly Don–style dress, a more stylish but still functional alternative to the shapeless Mother Hubbard–style housedresses that were omnipresent in the early 20th century.

The Tureman Mansion is now a beautiful backdrop for a multi-floor space that houses one of the world's largest collections of historic toys, as well as the world's largest fine-scale miniature collection. Two Kansas Citians—Mary Harris Francis and Barbara Hall Marshall—donated their personal collections to start the museum, which has since expanded twice and now includes 33,000 square feet of exhibit space. Make a complete tour of the museum and you'll see more than 93,000 objects—and that's not counting traveling exhibits that rotate every year.

"You know, I really feel that some people are born with a tendency to like small things . . . and I think I'm one of those," says Marshall in a video produced by the museum. "I think the thing that attracts me to pieces is the artistic effort that's put into them."

The museum's miniature collection includes everything from individual pieces of furniture, like a Queen Anne secretary desk that's not quite seven inches tall, carved in 1924; to impeccably detailed scenes like an Art Deco jewelry store, complete with browsing customers, and a perfectly scaled miniature of the Nelson-Atkins Museum of Art's entrance.

Upstairs, carefully curated exhibits trace the history of toys from early dolls and blocks to board games and zoetropes. Prepare for a rush of nostalgia in decade-themed exhibits that showcase beloved toys and collectibles from the mid-1900s to the turn of the 21st century. We'll toss just a few teasers your way: Etch A Sketch, Teddy Ruxpin, Nerf, Lego, and Strawberry Shortcake. One thing's for certain: This museum will reinforce that you're never too old to have fun.

This is one museum gift shop you won't want to miss. Take home a favorite childhood toy, locally made jewelry and art, or a fully stocked kit you can use to build your own detailed miniature scene.

A range of miniatures—from lifestyle scenes to fully furnished mansions—is on display in Kansas City.

1997

Oldest Jazz Memorabilia on Display

American Jazz Museum

1616 E 18th St., Kansas City, MO

Opened on September 5, 1997, the American Jazz Museum as an entity isn't necessarily a historic landmark. Yet the depth and breadth of jazz memorabilia contained inside—and the museum staff's critical work to maintain historic 18th and Vine live jazz venues like the Blue Room—make the museum a natural inclusion in a book like this.

Picture this for just a moment: On that September evening in 1997, a red carpet rolls down 18th and Vine. Renowned musicians like Billy Dee Williams, Dianne Reeves, Harry Belafonte, bandleader George Duke, Tony Bennett, Claude "Fiddler" Williams, Jay McShann, and Pat Metheny converge on this historic neighborhood for a three-day celebration that included a ticketed gala and a giant outdoor screen that broadcast the festivities for the surrounding community to see.

Inside the museum—a project more than 50 years in the making—you'll peruse an extensive array of jazz-themed exhibits. Iconic neon signs light the way as you move through the space, a nod to city streets of the past lined with live music venues and clubs. Learn more about iconic jazz performers, the instruments they loved, and the music they created with interactive exhibits that include listening booths.

The American Jazz Museum brings the concept of interactivity to new heights. The museum property includes the Blue Room, a live jazz club built in tribute to one of the neighborhood's historic nightspots. In the 1930s, the Blue

Immerse yourself in the interactive surroundings of the American Jazz Museum.

Room was the nightclub of the adjoining Street Hotel, listed in *The Negro Motorist Green Book* as a safe haven for black travelers (and where Jackie Robinson lived while he played for the Kansas City Monarchs).

During your museum visit, make sure you head outside to the eastern corner of Vine and East 17th Terrace (behind the museum). Here, you'll see one of Kansas City's most iconic sculptures: the face of Charlie "Bird" Parker, arguably the most important figure in Kansas City's jazz emergence and evolution. Robert Graham designed and created the statue, which was unveiled in March 1999.

The American Jazz Museum and the Negro Leagues Baseball Museum occupy the same building in 18th and Vine. Separate tickets are required for each museum (combo tickets may be available), but this is the easiest way to experience two important Kansas City museums in the same afternoon.

1500s/1844

Oldest Watering Hole and Campground

Cave Spring Park

8701 E Gregory Blvd., Kansas City, MO

As travelers made their way along the Santa Fe Trail throughout the 19th century (the commercial highway connected Missouri to Santa Fe, New Mexico), they might have stopped at Cave Spring Park to camp and to enjoy cold water from the park's namesake water source.

Let's take a moment, though, to acknowledge that Cave Spring Park and the surrounding land was likely occupied as early as the 1500s by Osage natives. Sac, Kansa, and Fox Indigenous peoples also camped here, one of many examples of land throughout Kansas City that knew a rich history and importance before settlers arrived in later decades.

By 1844, a man named Jesse Barnes owned the land and allowed wagon trains to stop and make camp. Later that century, the land's ownership changed to Solomon Young, Harry Truman's grandfather; then to Urban and Gladys Kroell, who opened a private country club on the property. The land would eventually be purchased by Kansas City's Klein family.

Klein family patriarch William H. Klein considered developing the 39-acre parcel. Vocal neighbors and Jackson County legislators instead convinced Klein to "establish a park and honor the historical significance of the trail," according to *The Kansas City Jewish Chronicle*. "All but the street-facing corner parcel was in the county's control at the time of Klein's passing in 1979, when the park was named in his honor. In the ensuing years, Klein's family never pursued the development of the last piece of the land." In fact, the family donated the remaining 3.4 acres to Jackson County in 2020.

"We always thought that in the end, we would complete the circle and donate this most visible tract to protect the integrity of the park," said one of Bill's three sons, James Klein, in an interview with the *KCJC*.

Today, Cave Spring Park is "a little hidden forest in the city," according to the Cave Spring Association. The 36-acre urban nature center and historic center is home to, yes, a cave, as well as a water garden, bird sanctuary, flower gardens, historic ruins, and a butterfly garden. A six-mile network of trails spreads out over the land; some of the trails are paved for full accessibility.

As part of its preservation and education work, the Cave Spring Association maintains a park website at cavespring.org where you can access a live Google map to accompany your self-guided tour.

Courtesy of Kansas City Parks & Recreation

Mid-1700s

Oldest Living Bur Oak Tree

Liberty Tree

328 S Monroe Ave., Kansas City, MO

When you think of the powerful thunderstorms and tornadoes that have raged through Kansas City in the last 200-plus years, it's incredible to think that a towering tree still thrives. Yet, in the yard next to a brick home in Kansas City's Historic Northeast, a bur oak tree might be approaching 260 years old . . . or even older.

A previous homeowner received a printed certificate commemorating the designation, which, along with a yard marker, remains with the home. Dated 1976, the certificate proclaimed the bur oak as a Liberty Tree, a "200-year-old living monument to our nation's history," wrote Vicky Diaz-Camacho for Flatland KC.

After an inquiry from Jones, Flatland's curiousKC team delved into the roots (pun intended) of the area's Liberty Trees. They were, in fact, part of a recognition program launched by the American Revolution Bicentennial Administration in 1976 to identify and celebrate bicentennial landmarks, including trees.

The Westport Oak tree on 43rd Street near Saint Luke's Hospital might have rivaled the Liberty Tree in age, but it was removed after suffering significant damage in a 2002 ice storm because it "posed a hazard for passersby," Diaz-Camacho wrote. A *Lawrence Journal-World* article detailed the tree's difficult history: it provided much-needed shade along the Santa Fe Trail, but was also used for pre–Civil War lynchings.

The Liberty Tree isn't just a likely candidate for the oldest tree in Kansas City; an arborist's 2019 inspection, cited by Flatland, also proclaimed the tree the largest that the inspector had seen to date.

In case you're headed to a tree-themed trivia night any time soon, bur oaks are dense shade trees that produce large acorns. They commonly live for 200 to 300 years, which means the Liberty Tree may still have several memory-making decades ahead.

The tree is located in the yard of a private residence, so please be respectful when exploring. The home is part of the Historic Northeast neighborhood, which means you're a short walk or drive from the Museum of Kansas City, Cliff Drive, and the city's first suburb, Pendleton Heights.

1931/2010

Oldest Airline Museum in Kansas City

The TWA Museum

10 Richards Rd., #110, Kansas City, MO

Kansas City International Airport is the Kansas City metro's regional, national, and international travel hub, yet aviation enthusiasts shouldn't pass up a trip to the Charles B. Wheeler Downtown Airport (MKC), built in 1927 and dedicated in a ceremony led by Charles Lindbergh.

Originally operating as the Kansas City Municipal Airport, the facility was renamed for two-time Kansas City mayor Charles Wheeler in 2001. Just as Kansas City's central location was ideal for riverboat and railroad traffic, MKC became a bustling hub of passenger airline traffic, putting Kansas City on its way to becoming the air capital of the United States.

Transcontinental Air Transport (TAT) and Western Air Express began running a new passenger terminal in 1928, and, by 1929 "Kansas City Municipal Airport was home to more passenger airlines than any other airport in the nation and had acquired the title, 'Air Hub of America,'" according to the airport. When TAT merged with Western Air Express and Maddux Airlines to become Transcontinental & Western Air, Inc., or TWA, Lindbergh helped secure Kansas City's selection as the airline's world headquarters.

Although TWA ceased operations in 2001, remnants of its history and impact on Kansas City are visible throughout the city, including within the TWA Museum, part of the downtown airport complex. The museum started with the extensive collection of Tom Perry, one of the airport's instrument shop mechanics, and opened in its current location in 2010.

Not only can you explore a wealth of TWA memorabilia, including photographs, travel posters, company uniforms, and more, but the museum also exhibits historic aircraft, including a 1937 Lockheed Electra 12A Junior. Experience a pilot's perspective in a variety of cockpit trainers and live the high life in a re-created Ambassador's Club, complete with furniture once owned by Howard Hughes.

For more TWA history, don't miss a stroll around TWA's former corporate headquarters at 1735 Baltimore Avenue in downtown Kansas City's Crossroads Arts District, now home to advertising firm BarkleyOKRP. You'll know you're in the right place when you spot a replica TWA Moonliner, the creation of TWA and the Walt Disney Company to imagine commercial flights to the moon.

Courtesy of Visit KC

1917

Oldest Local Hospital to Treat Black Patients

Wheatley Provident Hospital

1826 Forest Ave., Kansas City, MO

Courtesy of KCPL

Although this once-stately stone building is in significant disrepair, it's worth at least a driving-tour stop to recognize a local health-care landmark: Kansas City's first and only private hospital created to treat black patients.

Wheatley Provident Hospital's story began more than a century ago, when physician Dr. John Edward Perry moved to Kansas City from Columbia and founded both a medical treatment facility (for patients) and a training center (for doctors and nurses).

A community initiative—the New Movement Association—took over operations of Perry's facility and changed its name to the Provident Hospital and Nurse Training Association, according to the African-American Heritage Trail of Kansas City.

At the same time, Kansas Citian Phyllis Wheatley had launched a fundraising campaign to build a hospital for black patients. At the urging of the Board of Public Welfare, the two organizations merged in April 1914 and a newly elected board of directors named the resulting facility Wheatley Provident Hospital and Nurse Training Association. An ideal premises—

formerly the St. Joseph Catholic School—became available, and the hospital opened on Forest Avenue in 1917 in the heart of Kansas City's historic 18th and Vine neighborhood.

Unfortunately, the building has remained mostly vacant since the hospital closed in 1972 and moved to a different location. Much like the Kansas City Workhouse—located nearby at 2001 Vine Street and built in 1897—the Wheatley Provident Hospital building is an important reminder of not just local history but also the tenacity and triumph of black Kansas Citians.

Wheatley Provident Hospital and the Kansas City Workhouse are visible from the street, and trespassing on either property is prohibited. It's the author's sincere hope that thoughtful revitalization to both landmarks will be underway by the time you visit.

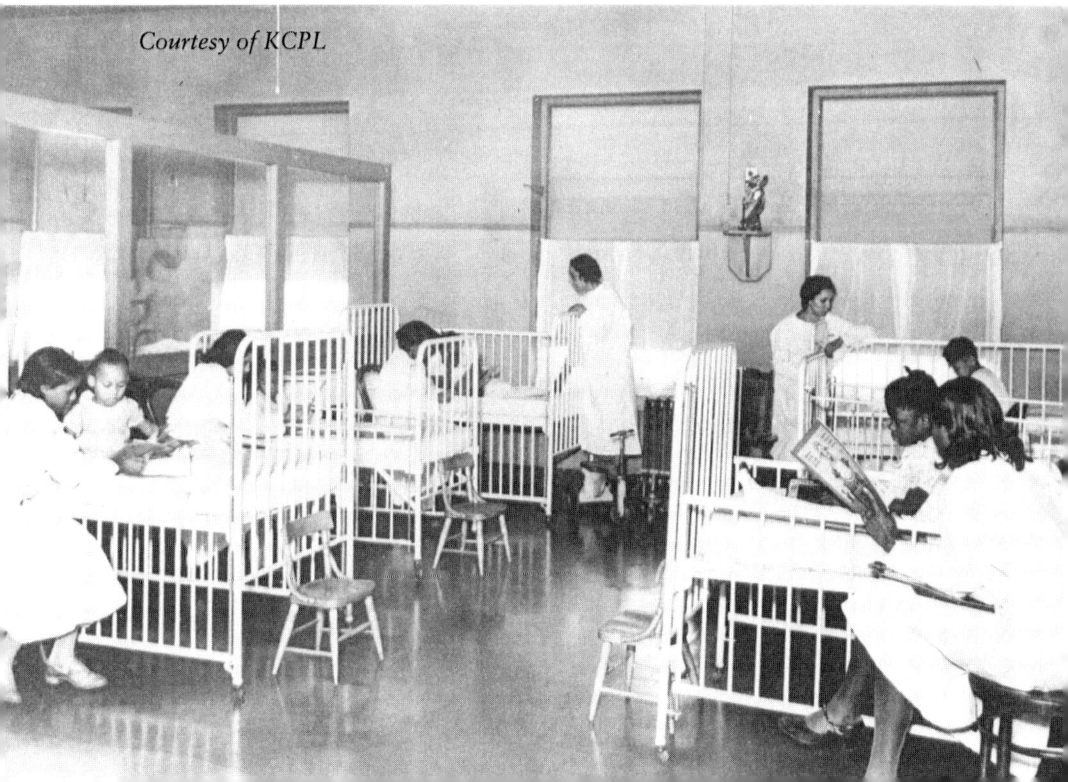

Courtesy of KCPL

1893

OLDEST NORTH–SOUTH BOULEVARD

THE PASEO

Kansas City's first boulevard began at Independence Avenue and progressed to 17th Street. The Paseo took its name from the Paseo de la Reforma in Mexico City, the design of which would inspire Kansas City's counterpart, which would eventually extend south to 79th Street.

Not only was the Paseo an integral part of George Kessler's parks and boulevards plan, but it also served as a key connector to the Parade, an 18-acre site between 15th and 18th Streets and Flora and Woodland Avenues. As the 20th century began, demand grew in cities for open land that could accommodate parades, public gatherings, and sports.

Parks and boulevard commissioners envisioned the Paseo as similar to Drexel Boulevard in Chicago, a parkway that "would act as a promenade connecting the Parade to the entire boulevard system," wrote Patrick Alley and Dona Boley in *Images of America: Kansas City's Parks and Boulevards*. "In each median between the numbered east–west streets would be a succession of flower gardens with water features, structures, walks, and landscaping. The Paseo would be the only city park where

Paseo stoplight in 1932. Courtesy of KCPL

Left: Historic view of Paseo YMCA. Right: Historic view of Paseo pergolas
Photos courtesy of KCPL

residents could see beautiful flowers in abundance, artistically displayed. Also, travelers going to and from downtown would pass by these oases of urban planning."

The Parade did, indeed, become a lively park. The open field was prone to flooding in colder months, transforming the land into a skating rink. Additional highlights of the Parade included a playground and the city's first public bath, complete with a shower, baths, and swimming pool. The public bathhouse became exclusively for use by black residents in 1919.

Another striking feature of the Paseo is the Pergola, a blocks-long structure that includes an open-latticed roof supported by fluted columns. This, along with other features like sunken gardens and Troost Lake, brought continuous streams of visitors and traffic to the Paseo. A description that accompanies a Paseo postcard, part of the Kansas City Public Library's Missouri Valley Special Collections, proclaimed that the Paseo was the most photographed part of Kansas City at the turn of the 20th century.

Look for Kansas City's first traffic light, which still stands at the Paseo and Linwood Boulevard.

1949

Oldest Still-Operating Mexican Restaurant

Los Corrals

408 W 9th St., Kansas City, MO

Perched just a few blocks away from the restaurant's current location, Los Corrals opened in 1949 and now occupies a downtown Kansas City building that dates back to 1889.

You'll find a menu filled with Mexican staples: flautas, tostadas, and enchiladas. But if you want a literal taste of history, order fried tacos. Sure, Kansas City loves its barbecue. But we have our own style of taco, too, and Los Corrals was the first restaurant to sell it.

As José Ralat wrote for Eater.com, Kansas City–style street tacos were created by Luis Silva, founder of Spanish Gardens Taco House (now operating as food manufacturer Spanish Gardens Foods), the "result of the proximity of the area's Italian and Mexican communities." Stuffed with seasoned beef, the fried tacos are "topped with a ketchup-like 'taco sauce' and Parmesan cheese," a preferred choice since Parmesan was plentiful and easy to get.

And that's the way you'll get them at Los Corrals—piping hot, filled with your choice of protein (beef, chicken, or beans) and topped either tostada or chalupa style. The tacos sound simple, but they take time to prepare because of their stuffed proportions. Some restaurants prefer to make and sell faster tacos, as Ralat discovered, but a number of local restaurants join Los Corrals in offering the Kansas City staple: P.R.'s Place, a Westside bar that opened in 1974; Manny's, a family-owned Crossroads favorite since 1980; and Ponak's Mexican Kitchen

& Bar, which opened on Southwest Boulevard in 1975 and might serve the strongest margaritas in the city.

A fun fact about Los Corrals? It's next door to Kansas City's oldest bar and grill, the Peanut, which operated pre-Prohibition as a speakeasy. Pro tip: Host your own food crawl with an order of Kansas City–style tacos and a draft margarita from Los Corrals, followed by a plate of spicy, saucy chicken wings at the Peanut. Now that's a delicious day!

Local fast-food landmark the Northland's In-A-Tub serves its own take on the Kansas City taco, replacing Parmesan with a "neon orange powdered cheese," wrote Claudia Brancart for KCUR. In-A-Tub—or just "the Tub"—has operated since 1951 and is located at 4000 North Oak Trafficway, Kansas City.

Courtesy of Los Corrals

Kansas City, KS, and Wyandotte County

ca. 1843

OLDEST PRIVATE CEMETERY

WYANDOT NATIONAL BURYING GROUND

631 Minnesota Ave.

More than 600 members of the Wyandot Nation left their homes in the Lake Huron region of Ohio and Michigan, opting to undertake a grueling and dangerous journey in exchange for Kansas lands promised by the federal government.

Heartbreak awaited the travelers on their 1843 arrival. Not only had the promised lands been claimed by others, but anywhere from 50 to 100 Wyandot Nation people died during the journey. The surviving members were left with a small piece of land near the Kaw River, deemed too risky of a location to bury their dead.

Instead, the group found a nearby hilltop that, today, is located in the heart of downtown Kansas City, Kansas. The deceased members of Wyandot Nation were buried, but as development of the area rose to an explosive pitch, the coveted hillside location caught the eyes of developers and city leaders.

Legal fights began, with an initial victory secured by three women of Wyandot Nation lineage: Lyda, Helena, and Ida Conley. They armed themselves and maintained active watch in the burying ground while they also led a legal challenge that eventually reached the Supreme Court.

"[The Conley sisters] made the decision to live at the cemetery in a small shelter, wielding shotguns and demonstrating their resolve

to use their weapons against any who would trespass on the cemetery,” according to an account published by theclio.com. “They maintained this resistance for two years, an action that proved vital to preventing the sale and commercial development of the cemetery.”

Although the sisters achieved victory (and Lyda Conley became the first Indigenous woman to argue a case to the Supreme Court), additional legal challenges ensued over subsequent decades. It would take more than a century for the burying ground to achieve official and nonnegotiable protection through a combination of legal victories, as well as designations on the National Register of Historic Places in 1971 and as a National Historic Landmark in 2016.

The cemetery grew to serve as the sacred final resting place for 600 to 800 people of Wyandot Nation descent.

Among Indigenous burial grounds, Wyandot National Burying Ground (part of Huron Park) is one that does allow public pedestrian access. Please take care not to disturb any signage or burial markers and maintain a respectful, reflective mindset during your visit. Access points next to the Kansas City, Kansas, Public Library may be closed; enter the Wyandot National Burying Ground on 7th Street.

1857

Oldest Home in Wyandotte County

Grinter Place

1420 S 78th St., Kansas City, KS

As more than 100,000 Indigenous people were forced from their homes in the East to reservations west of the Mississippi River between 1825 and 1843, some of them may have ridden on a ferry across the Kansas River operated by Kentuckian Moses Grinter.

Grinter married a Lenape (Delaware) woman, Annie Marshall, whose family had been forcibly relocated to the Fort Leavenworth Indian Agency in the early 1830s. In addition to working as a ferry operator, Grinter ran a trading post from 1855 to 1860 and supplied a wide assortment of goods to Delaware Indians in exchange for cash and furs, according to the Kansapedia at kansashistory.gov.

In the midst of that period—1857—Annie and Moses built their brick farmstead, which overlooks the Kansas River's Delaware Crossing. The home remained in the Grinter family through significant historic events like Kansas statehood, the Civil War, and brisk settler traffic as westward expansion captivated the country.

Moses and Annie's great-granddaughter sold the estate in 1950 to Harry and Bernice Hanson, who operated a restaurant specializing in fried chicken dinners out of the home until the 1960s. Here's an excerpt

Courtesy of Grinter Place Friends, Inc.

from the March 12, 1950, *Kansas City Star* ad that the Hansons answered, as detailed by Grinter Place Friends, Inc:

Courtesy of Grinter Place Friends, Inc.

"Old homestead—7 room brick with 5 fireplaces. High and slightly overlooking Kansas river. 19.5 acres, large horse barn. Ideal for country home, ten minutes to city. Bonner Springs bus line."

With the help of the Junior League of Kansas City, Kansas, and the Grinter Place Friends, the state of Kansas acquired the Grinters' estate in 1971, and it has since been the site of the Grinter Place Historic Site, operated by the Grinter Place Friends, Inc.

Visit the site and you'll not only see three buildings—the Visitor's Center, the Shelter House, and the Historic Site—but you can also explore the property's walking trail, revived by hardworking volunteers in 2016 who cleared abundant overgrowth to create an easily navigable trail that also offers prime bird-watching.

Grinter Place isn't far from western Wyandotte County, which in recent decades has seen a flurry of economic development resulting in newer landmarks like NASCAR's Kansas Speedway, a major-league soccer stadium, Children's Mercy Park, and a mixed-use retail and dining district known as the Legends at Village West. This outdoor outlet mall also serves as a picturesque walking route with signage that calls attention to native plants and historically significant Kansans.

Oldest Privately Owned Bowling Alley

St. John's Catholic Club

414 Barnett Ave., Kansas City, KS

Who would suspect a basement bowling alley awaits inside?

Croatian immigrants living in the Kansas City, Kansas, neighborhood of Strawberry Hill established the St. John the Baptist parish in 1900, and construction of St. John the Baptist Church was complete in 1904 with the blessing of the building's cornerstone. The church itself is a beautiful example of international collaboration, featuring Austrian-made altars and pulpit and stained-glass windows created in Switzerland.

The church's basement hall quickly became a busy place for meetings and social gatherings. Demand soon exceeded available space, prompting parishioners to create a separate neighboring building: St. John's Catholic Club, purpose-built for recreation and fellowship. The two-story building included lower-level club rooms and an upper-level auditorium and was completed in 1925.

Sports and recreational activities proved among the most popular reasons to gather at the club, which was initially outfitted with two bowling lanes and two billiard tables. Bowling grew so popular that additional lanes were purchased in 1939 and 1947, leading to the creation of weeknight bowling leagues in a place you might least expect them.

The club's six lanes were replaced in 2012 and continue to operate today for Catholic Club members and for private event bookings. Celebrating the church's Croatian roots is an ongoing priority for the parish, but the Catholic Club and its neighboring church are open to all.

"It's a place to gather and it doesn't matter what your religion is," said St. John's Catholic Club Chairman Jaime Clark in a 2020 article published by Flatland KC. "It's just a place where you feel safe. It's a comfort spot."

Oh, and fun fact: Yes, the church bowling alley includes a bar—bowling does create quite a thirst, after all! Leagues continue to meet at the bowling alley throughout a season spanning from Labor Day through March—the best time of year to gather inside and avoid cold Kansas City winters. Should you have an opportunity to bowl a game, be prepared to keep score the traditional way: with paper and pencil.

An unexpected encounter: Cue up Queer Eye *season 4, episode 5, titled "On Golden Kenny." You'll meet Kenny Yarnevich, a St. John's parishioner who is a frequent fixture behind the bar in the Catholic Club and helps keep the club in tip-top shape.*

1887/1988

Oldest Queen-Anne-Mansion-Turned-Museum

Strawberry Hill Ethnic Cultural Society

720 N 4th St., Kansas City, KS

This luxurious and meticulously appointed Queen Anne–style mansion, which was constructed in 1887 as the dream home for John and Margaret Scroggs (along with Margaret's children from her previous marriage), was sold in 1919 and became St. John's Orphanage, operated by the Sisters of St. Francis of Christ the King in connection with St. John the Baptist Catholic Church.

A sudden, devastating need for the orphanage emerged in 1918 when a number of local children lost their parents during the vicious influenza pandemic. The orphanage would continue operations until 1988, when it closed and the Cruise-Scroggs Mansion converted to the Strawberry Hill Ethnic Cultural Society.

This stately hilltop home contains rooms of exhibits that celebrate the incredible array of cultural populations living in the Strawberry Hill neighborhood of Kansas City, Kansas, originally known as Splitlog Hill when it was purchased by Mathias Splitlog in 1870. Represented ethnicities include Croatian, Danish, Lithuanian, Dutch, Polish, Russian, Slovakian, Slovenian, and Ukrainian.

In addition to exploring culturally significant artifacts, clothing, art, and more, the Strawberry Hill Ethnic Culture Society offers a busy events calendar that enables cultural immersion through cooking classes and rotating themed exhibits. Each year the museum closes in late November so that hardworking volunteers can transform the mansion into a Christmas wonderland, a beautiful sight you won't soon forget.

We don't want to spoil your trip through the museum, but here's a sneak preview of the exhibits you'll see. Through a glass viewing area, you can see the bed that was installed on a TWA plane commissioned for Pope John Paul II. The pope "used the bed on three visits to the United States: in 1979, 1987, and 1995," Alex Smith wrote for KCUR. "Between visits and after his final trip, the bed was stored at a TWA facility in Kansas City." Local clergyman Rev. John Horvat insisted the bed be included in the museum in recognition of the pope's Polish heritage.

Strawberry Hill is absolutely worth an entire day of your attention. The vibrant, dense neighborhood includes a collection of businesses, restaurants, bars, and churches—lots of churches. Notable stops include St. John's Park for one of the best Kansas City skyline views; Slap's BBQ, a current front-runner for the area's favorite barbecue restaurant; Flagship Books; and specialty coffee shop Kinship Café. The KCK Legacy Trail audio tour is also a great companion on a self-guided exploration, available at kcklegacytrail.com.

OLDEST REMNANTS OF THE UNDERGROUND RAILROAD

QUINDARO RUINS

3421 N 29th St., Kansas City, KS

As the Kansas Territory expanded in the 1850s, Quindaro joined towns like Lawrence and Topeka in declaring their ardent Free Soil stance.

While on a barge scouting possible port town locations along the Missouri River between Kansas City and Leavenworth, Kansas, Charles Robinson spotted "a natural levy with a level rock ledge and deep water, providing easy and safe portage for steamboats and said to be the best landing on the Missouri River," wrote Tony O'Bryan for the Border War Encyclopedia.

Courtesy of Visit Kansas City, Kansas

The Wyandot Nation owned the land and sold it to Robinson with the help of Abelard Guthrie, whose wife, Nancy Quindaro Guthrie, was the daughter of a Wyandot Nation chieftain. (Trivia note: The name "Quindaro" translates to "bundle of sticks.")

After an 1857 groundbreaking, Quindaro soon grew to include a large population of residents, including freed African Americans. They, along with town residents and members of the Wyandot Nation, helped enslaved people escaping Missouri flee into Kansas.

Courtesy of Visit Kansas City, Kansas

"At times, they confronted slave catchers directly and refused to cooperate in returning runaways to their owners," O'Bryan wrote. "More often they secretly and quietly fed, hid and sheltered the escapees on their journey to freedom. The nearby Quindaro-Parkville ferry is said to have made clandestine night runs, causing the pro-slavery side to sink it in frustration in 1861. Undeterred in their pursuit of freedom, some of the enslaved people boldly walked across the Missouri River to freedom in Kansas during the unusually cold winter of 1862 when the ice formed a solid sheet."

Although economic growth in Quindaro drastically slowed following the Civil War and the town was all but abandoned, revitalization eventually took place. The bluff-top Quindaro Freedmen's School became Western University in 1881, the earliest black college west of the Mississippi River and the only one in Kansas. Education continued to play an important role in

Quindaro; in 1911, residents erected a statue of abolitionist John Brown holding a diploma "as an indication of their gratitude for his sacrifice and as a symbol of their faith in education as a means toward progress for African Americans." Brown's likeness is the oldest remaining statue in the Kansas City area.

Today, the Quindaro Ruins Townsite Project undertakes preservation of and education about the structural elements that remain of Quindaro and Western University, site of the first black ROTC program. Guided tours are recommended and can be booked at quindaroruinsprojectfoundationkck.org.

Lisa Peña is the founder of Urban Hikes KC, which offers a variety of guided hiking tours that offer deeper immersion into some of Kansas City's most historic and significant neighborhoods. One of several Kansas City, Kansas-focused routes is the Quindaro Ruins Urban Hike, an approximately three-mile route that includes hills and rocky terrain. Details at urbanhikeskc.com.

1977

Oldest Continuously Running Festival

Kansas City Renaissance Festival

633 N 130th St., Bonner Springs, KS

One of the largest Renaissance festivals in the US kicks off in late August in Bonner Springs, bringing medieval-era revelry and feasting to crowds of around 200,000 people.

The festival started in 1977 as a small fundraiser for the Kansas City Art Institute before growing into a stand-alone event in the late 1990s.

Each year, fairgrounds in Bonner Springs are transformed into a 16th-century English village complete with shops, restaurants, and live entertainment ranging from jousting to magic shows. Performers roam the village streets, delighting visitors with talents like juggling, fire eating, and of course, period-appropriate costumes.

Courtesy of the Kansas City Renaissance Festival

KC Ren Fest is held over several fall weekends, and each weekend includes a themed experience. Are you passionate about pirates? You'll love the High Seas Adventure. Irish enthusiasts, try the Celtic Celebration. Or get ready for spooky season during Halloween Daze and Spooky Knights.

A must-try during the festival? Freshly roasted turkey leg, the unofficial food of medieval villages everywhere. Wash down your turkey feast with a mug of ale and you'll be fueled for more medieval mischief.

One of the most incredible parts of KC Ren Fest is the sheer number of performers required to create such an entertaining and immersive experience. Each year, auditions are held to find actors, dancers, musicians, and other types of performance artists. Among the longest tenured? Rod Sipe, a fire eater and magician who's worked at Ren Fest since 1979, one of three performers to achieve such a lengthy tenure.

Courtesy of the Kansas City Renaissance Festival

Groups of performers will gather at other notable annual events like the KC St. Patrick's Day Parade for merrymaking and crowd interaction, all in the name of building anticipation for that year's Ren Fest season. You're never too old for fairy tales; and KC Ren Fest feels like a storybook come to life.

Pro tip: Wear comfortable shoes, bring cash, and stash layers or rain gear in case of changing weather conditions. The Kansas City Renaissance Festival is open rain or shine! Full festival details at kcrenfest.com.

Independence, MO

1898

Oldest Soda Fountain to Employ Harry S. Truman

Clinton's Soda Fountain

100 W Maple Ave., Independence, MO

The traditional soda fountain (no, not the machines you use at the gas station) and the role of the soda jerk are increasingly hard to find—except in Independence.

Part of the charming downtown surrounding the historic Independence Square, Clinton's Soda Fountain is much more than a place to enjoy a refreshing phosphate or a hand-scooped milkshake.

In this building—the former home of Clinton's Drugstore, built in the late 1800s—14-year-old Harry Truman had his first job around 1898. According to the building's historical marker, business owner Jim Clinton paid Truman a salary of $3 per week for work that included opening the store, mopping floors, taking out trash, and cleaning and operating the soda fountain, according to the Harry S. Truman Library and Museum.

"[That payment] was the biggest thing that happened to me," Truman recalled in his memoirs, "and my father told me to save it for myself when I tried to give it to him on coming home that Saturday night."

Sadly, like so many early buildings, the original Clinton's Drugstore succumbed to fire damage in 1906. A second building was constructed and the drugstore reopened, drawing steady streams of visitors who, over time, have represented all 50 states.

Subsequent decades saw a number of businesses in the building, including a shoe store and jewelry shop. Clinton's Soda Fountain revived the soda fountain part of Clinton's Drugstore's business model, opening in 1988. Stop in today and you'll immediately notice a carefully preserved interior that the owners have kept as intact as possible. The marble countertop that spans the soda fountain is more than 100 years old. The bar's wooden backdrop and shelves are reclaimed from a similar business in Kansas. And historic photographs displayed on the walls create a visual time capsule of Independence history.

You can't go wrong with Harry's Favorite, a butterscotch sundae with chocolate ice cream. Clinton's is closed Sundays, Mondays, and significant holidays, but operates year-round.

Oldest Government Building in Jackson County

1827 Log Courthouse

107 W Kansas Ave., Independence, MO

Courtesy of the City of Independence

How's this for perspective: Once this log courthouse was built by slave labor in 1827, it stood as the "only courthouse between Independence and the Pacific Ocean for more than 40 years," according to the City of Independence.

Jackson County, home to Kansas City, Missouri, began developing before the Town of Kansas was incorporated in 1850. Independence was established in 1827, and the log courthouse is one of the few structures still standing from the city's founding.

The building didn't immediately start as a courthouse, however. Funded by Mormon convert Algernon Sidney (A.S.) Gilbert, the building first served as Gilbert's home and store. Six years later, Jackson County citizens forcibly evicted Gilbert (and all other Mormons) from the city and seized their property.

"There are historical records of the formal declaration that banishes all Mormons from Jackson County in July 1833," wrote Mary-Lynn Pell for theclio.com. "The order occurred among increasing violence between non-Mormon vigilantes and Mormons."

Courtesy of the Historic Marker Database

After Gilbert fled north of the Missouri River to Clay County (where he was later killed), the log structure became a courthouse, providing "the earliest forms of government service and the last of civilization that many would see for years to come," Pell wrote.

Estimates indicate that anywhere from 300,000 to 500,000 settlers started their journeys west from this courthouse. President Harry S. Truman served as a judge until the early 1930s. At some point soon after, the city's judicial operations moved to a brick courthouse built on the Independence Square in 1836. Truman led the construction of the current courthouse, completed in 1933.

Tours of the 1827 Log Courthouse are available by appointment: 816-325-7575. The Jackson County Historical Society is also an enriching stop inside the Historic Truman Courthouse at 112 West Lexington Avenue.

1919

Oldest Family-Owned Restaurant

Dixon's Famous Chili

9105 E US Hwy. 40, Independence, MO

Courtesy of Dixon's Chili

Kansas City history includes a number of people who started selling food from pushcarts or otherwise no-frills street setups and went on to open their own brick-and-mortar restaurants. That includes Vergne Dixon, who started his chili business in 1919 at the restaurant's original location near downtown Independence.

You might have heard of Kansas City–style barbecue, but what about KC-style chili? Here's a primer from Sylvia Maria Gross, a reporter for local NPR affiliate KCUR. "[The chili] is not tomato-based, the beans and meat are cooked separately, and it's served on a plate. The condiments are do-it-yourself. You can choose from: onions, a jalapeno relish, vinegar, hot sauce, cheese and sour cream. If you want it a little wetter, you can get your chili 'soupy' with extra bean broth, or 'juicy,' with grease that was squeezed out of the meat." (If you happen to hear a regular customer order their chili "greasy," that's what the style was first called before Dixon's management changed the term to something more palatable).

Of course, it's not Dixon's chili without the restaurant's signature chili powder, a closely guarded family recipe.

Courtesy of Dixon's Chili

In more recent years, ketchup became part of the condiment line-up once Vergne wasn't around to see it happen. In his day, topping chili with ketchup was downright blasphemous, and he would charge customers a nickel for the request.

At one point, family-owned Dixon's became a full-fledged franchise with 13 locations, including a Minnesota restaurant. Slowly, 12 of the locations closed over time, leaving the last remaining location on Highway 40 in Independence. Stephen Steffes, Vergne's great-great-nephew, is now at the Dixon's helm as manager; his mother, Terri Totta-Smith, is the owner.

Like other historic businesses throughout Independence, Dixon's once counted Harry Truman among their customers, along with beloved local broadcaster Walt Bodine.

The "loose meat" texture described above is the hallmark of Kansas City–style chili. And this type of seasoned meat is available in other preparations, too. Another Independence eatery, a true drive-in called Mugs Up, has served their signature Zip burgers and frosty mugs of homemade root beer since 1956.

1899

Oldest Burger Joint

Courthouse Exchange

113 W Lexington Ave., Independence, MO

What's a better spot for a burger and beer joint than close to a municipal courthouse? Courthouse Exchange, located across the street from the historic Truman Courthouse, has beckoned with juicy burgers and cold beer since father-and-son duo Joseph Poggenpohl and Joseph Poggenpohl Jr. opened the eatery in 1899.

Once you enter the restaurant, you descend beneath the street to seating enclosed by rock walls and a wooden bar. Even a basic lunch becomes somewhat clandestine in this literal hidden gem. If you prefer your fun at street level, patio seating is also available.

Through the decades, the Courthouse Exchange has changed owners and locations, but the commitment to burgers and brews remains the same. Despite its proximity to the courthouse, a drama-filled robbery unfolded at the restaurant in 1909, according to a story by Hannah Bailey for NPR affiliate KCUR.

Courtesy of the City of Independence

"After forcing their way into the building, robbers blew up the safe and stole $150 before escaping," Bailey wrote.

The Courthouse Exchange has operated in its current below-street location since the 1970s, serving up comforting go-to's like fried chicken, pork tenderloin sandwiches, and a build-your-own baked potato.

Keep an eye on the Courthouse Exchange website, courthouseexchange.com, if your visit falls during the summer. June kicks off the restaurant's Between the Bricks live music series, featuring weekly performers through September.

The Courthouse Exchange brings new meaning to the term "drink local." In addition to a varied beer menu, the restaurant also stocks Independence-made Polly's Pop. If you find a flavor you love, the brand's retail store is a four-minute walk from the Courthouse Exchange.

Courtesy of the Courthouse Exchange

1881

OLDEST VICTORIAN MANSION

VAILE VICTORIAN MANSION

1500 N Liberty St., Independence, MO

When Colonel and Mrs. Harvey Vaile unveiled their Second Empire–style mansion in 1881, *The Kansas City Times* proclaimed it "the most princely house and the most comfortable home in the entire west."

Courtesy of KCPL

Just one mile north of the historic Independence Square, the 31-room mansion designed by local architect Asa B. Cross wasn't just astoundingly ornate; it was also equipped with cutting-edge modern conveniences including a kitchen with indoor hot and cold running water, flushing toilets, and a 48,000-gallon wine cellar.

Italianate and Gothic details fill the home, including a main parlor fireplace adorned with hand-carved Cararra marble from Italy. Onyx accent pillars added a stark contrast to the snow-white marble and were said to "radiate with the glow from the fire," according to the Vaile Victorian Society. A solid black walnut grand staircase welcomed visitors as they entered the mansion through a vestibule, and painted ceilings helped visitors feel enveloped in art.

When the Vailes died, they left much of their estate to the Kansas City Ladies College, which proved financially unable to maintain the mansion. Ownership first changed to Carrie Mae Carrol Sprague, who operated the mansion as an inn, sanitarium and nursing home, and then to Mary Mildred DeWitt, president of the Jackson County Historical Society from 1961 to 1963, and her husband, J. Roger.

By this point, the Vaile Mansion teetered on the brink of demolition. The DeWitts began with an exterior renovation before turning their attention to the estate's interior. Before her death, Mary Mildred DeWitt succeeded in adding the mansion to the National Register of Historic Places; when she passed, she deeded the house and surrounding grounds to the City of Independence.

The Victorian Society of the Vaile Mansion-DeWitt Museum formed in 1983 and led extensive renovations of the property, adding museum exhibits that detail Victorian life and ensuring that the mansion's interior is furnished to accurately reflect the Victorian era.

Each June, the Victorian Society hosts the Strawberry Festival, which transforms the estate's grounds into a lively mix of vendors and entertainment reminiscent of a Victorian fair. Traveler's note: The mansion closes for the season on New Year's Eve and reopens again in the spring.

1859

OLDEST AREA JAIL

1859 JAIL MUSEUM

217 N Main St., Independence, MO

When the Asa Beebe Cross–designed 1859 Jail was built, it was the third jail built in Jackson County. The modest yet thoroughly fortified building included a home for the jailer, an office for the county marshal and his staff, and 12 limestone jail cells.

One of those cells would be occupied for 112 days by notorious bank robber Frank James, Jesse's brother. His cell was furnished with a Brussels carpet, fine furniture, and paintings. Not only did he have free run of the jail, he also hosted nightly card games.

What would land you in jail before the Civil War? The Jackson County Historical Society compiled several examples:

- Horse racing on public streets
- Firing guns in town
- Operating a gaming house
- Assault and battery
- Disturbing the peace (or a religious meeting)
- Building a privy "not over a pit"

Courtesy of the 1859 Jail Museum

Courtesy of the 1859 Jail Museum

After the Civil War, crimes escalated and most prisoners were held for murder, theft, assault, or kidnapping. A 1907 expansion added a brick cell block with 28 cells. The jail closed in 1920 by order of Judge Ralph Latshaw, Jackson County Criminal Court, to cut county costs. The jail was converted into a county workspace administered by the Community Welfare League and, during the Great Depression, by the Works Progress Administration. Finally, the building served as the meeting spot for American Legion Tirey J. Ford Post 21 until the building reached an extreme state of neglect and was nearly demolished.

The Jackson County Historical Society acquired the building in 1958 and has operated it as a museum since. Today, the jail is recognized as the oldest structure on the historic Independence Square.

The 1859 Jail Museum is open April through October and on December weekends. The museum is also home to the Jackson County Historical Society Store, a treasure trove of historic books and gifts.

Suburbs

1849

Oldest Private College or University

William Jewell College

500 College Hill, Liberty, MO

It's close, but William Jewell College in Liberty takes the title of oldest private college or university in the Kansas City metro, opening in 1849 as a Baptist men's college.

Dr. William Jewell—physician, legislator, and Baptist layman—provided initial funds and donated land to build the college, which was completed as a result of grassroots fundraising.

Classes were suspended during the Civil War, and Union Army members occupied campus to use Jewell Hall as "a lookout point, infirmary and stable," according to a historical account on the college's website.

The college reopened after the Civil War, and in 1920 began welcoming women students to the college population. William Jewell cultivated a reputation as a national liberal arts college that garnered attention for its "rigorous curriculum and outstanding student outcomes."

One of the college's most beloved initiatives, the Harriman-Jewell Series, started in 1965 as a partnership between English professors Richard Harriman and Dean Dunham Jr. They wanted to give students the opportunity to see the world's top performing artists (for free!), and the series continues today.

Gano Chapel. Courtesy of Yates Gill Union

Notable past performers include Luciano Pavarotti, who made his professional concert debut in 1973; cellist Yo-Yo Ma; and mezzo-soprano Joyce DiDonato. The current season calendar is available at hjseries.org.

As a more critical examination of history becomes increasingly common, even demanded, William Jewell College joined the Consortium of Universities Studying Slavery as part of a thorough racial reconciliation effort that began in 2020.

"From 1848 through 1865, William Jewell College benefitted from the talents, free labor and brilliance of enslaved Africans," according to the college's statement of atonement. "It is well-established that Jewell not only condoned and profited from the institution of slavery, but in some cases defended its horrendous practice. It is also evident that Jewell benefitted from discriminatory practices following slavery's abolition, even into the 21st century." One result of this work is the college's Slavery, Memory, and Justice Project, created by students and faculty in 2020 to answer several questions through research. Explore their work at slaverymemoryandjustice.org.

The William Jewell College campus is a roughly five-minute drive from historic downtown Liberty, site of the Jesse James Bank Museum and home to several more museums, shops, and restaurants, along with a Saturday farmers market from May through October.

1840/2016

Oldest Bed-and-Breakfast

Main Street Inn

504 Main St., Parkville, MO

Welcome to Parkville, a picturesque hamlet northwest of Kansas City. Founded in 1840 by Colonel George S. Park, Parkville offers a glimpse into the past with hilly, mostly brick streets lined with shops, historic homes, restaurants, and businesses.

One such business, the Main Street Inn, is the oldest bed-and-breakfast in the area, beating St. Joseph's Whiskey Mansion by just one year. The 5,000-square-foot Queen Anne mansion took two years to build, with construction complete in 1877. Parkville businessman J. E. Threlkeld was the home's first occupant, followed by another businessman and former postmaster, John Bueneman.

Jason and Kathy Ayers purchased the home in 2016 and oversaw a complete renovation to repair the home after extensive smoke damage from a fire next door. The Ayers channeled their architectural backgrounds to balance the home's historic features, including original wood floors, vibrant stained glass, and Queen Anne furnishings with colorful, modern design elements like handcrafted art pieces and recessed lighting.

Choose from three guest suites at Main Street Inn, two of which are named for legendary Parkville residents. The Col. Park Suite is a luxuriously inviting nod to Parkville's founder. Numerous windows offer prime views of Park's vision, including downtown's Main Street. The exposed brick wall

Photos courtesy of Main Street Inn

is original to the house and provides a beautifully preserved backdrop that frames the en suite jacuzzi.

The Old Kate room is named for the beloved mule that served Park University for almost three decades. When the university was first built, the campus included a farm where students could work to earn money to pay their tuitions. The standard-sized room is much like its namesake: practical, comfortable, and hardworking. Stay here and you'll be close to one of the home's favorite features, a wraparound veranda-style porch that's a fitting spot to start or end your day.

Lastly, the Missouri River suite is as eye-catching as its namesake and also features 1885 original brick walls and an en suite Jacuzzi. Skylights shower the suite in natural light, and a secluded balcony offers an effortless transition to the outdoors.

Oh, and about breakfast? Every guest enjoys a three-course meal that starts with homemade bread and French-pressed coffee delivered to your room, followed by fruit and a hot breakfast in the inn's dining room.

Have you started packing?

Fun fact: Not only did Old Kate inspire a room at Main Street Inn, but she has her own trail, too. The 0.9-mile loop is considered easy and offers abundant scenery throughout the Parkville Nature Sanctuary, including a bubbling waterfall, a boardwalk, and the Riss Lake dam.

1866

Oldest-Known Bank Robbed in Daylight, Peacetime

Jesse James Bank Museum

103 N Water St., Liberty, MO

History teaches us to recognize both the good and bad, right? Travel about 20 minutes north of Kansas City to Liberty to see the Jesse James Bank Museum, which memorializes the site of the country's first daylight, peacetime (post–Civil War) bank robbery on February 13, 1866. Yes, really.

"It was a cold and snowy February afternoon when a group of horsemen rode into Liberty, Missouri," according to an account by Clay County Tourism. "After a short time, gunshots broke the winter silence as the men rode off with their loot, leaving one young college student dead and the town in shock."

The building's evolution into a museum has helped keep the 1866 bank interior relatively intact. Experience the story as it unfolded from a bank-teller narrator and examine carefully preserved artifacts, including the bank's original green vault.

"Among the furnishings, a rare Seth Thomas clock, one of only two known to exist, hangs on the wall set for the exact

Courtesy of Clay County

time and date of the robbery," the Clay County Tourism account continues. A brief aside: Seth Thomas is the longest established clockmaker in the US, started by its namesake in the early 1800s in Connecticut. Thomas moved to another Connecticut town, Plymouth, and partnered with Eli Terry and Silas Hoadley to produce clocks at wholesale rates. The designs—known at the time as "hang-up" clocks, would become the grandfather clocks we still know today.

Original safe at the Jesse James Bank Museum. Courtesy of Clay County

During the robbery, James made off with $60,000 in a combination of "bonds, paper currency and gold and silver coin," according to PBS. The robbers were never caught and the money never recovered, a loss that ended up closing Clay County Savings and Loan just eight years after it opened. James would continue to rob banks for the next 15 years, eluding authorities. A member of James's gang, Charlie Ford, and his brother, Bob, decided to kill James and earn a lucrative reward from Missouri Governor Thomas Crittendon. Bob fired the fatal shot in James's living room on April 3, 1882.

Make it a Jesse James–themed day and travel approximately 25 minutes to Kearney, Missouri, to visit James's birthplace, an 1822 log cabin; James's grave site; and the world's largest display of James family artifacts. More information available at jessejamesmuseum.org.

5000 BC

OLDEST LOCAL HOME OF THE HOPEWELL CULTURE

RENNER-BRENNER SITE PARK

2901 NW Vivion Rd., Riverside, MO

Courtesy of the City of Riverside

Talk about a trip into the past. Riverside's Renner-Brenner Site Park was once home to a local population of the Hopewell culture around 5000 BC (and possibly earlier), according to a National Register of Historic Places marker built in 1987.

"Hopewell villages lay along rivers and streams," as detailed in the *Encyclopaedia Brittanica*. "The inhabitants raised corn (maize) and possibly beans and squash but still relied upon hunting and fishing and the gathering of wild nuts, fruits, seeds and roots."

Hopewell people were known for cultivating an extensive trading network—a harbinger of the many trading posts and exchanges that would later spring up in the Kansas City area. Remains of items traded by Hopewell people, including Gulf of Mexico seashells and shark's teeth discovered along the shores of Chesapeake Bay, show just how far across North America they traveled.

The discovery of relics by amateur archaeologist J. Mett Shippee and Smithsonian Institute assistant curator of archaeology Waldo R. Wedel in 1921 led to an understanding of just how long this area had been inhabited. Based on unearthed pottery fragments from this and other sites, historians think the Kansas City Hopewell may have migrated to the area from modern-day Illinois and, previously, what is now Ohio.

"Together, their findings indicated a significant abundance of prehistoric village debris corresponding to the eastern influence of the Woodland culture," according to the City of Riverside's City History examination, undertaken in part by residents Dale Garrison and Betty Burch. "Until their findings, it was thought that the Woodland Culture had not extended farther west than the Mississippi River."

Brenner family descendant Gary Brenner has been active in discovering and protecting the park's history, from unearthing relics in the early 1980s to maintaining an extensive digital record of the land and its people at RennerBrennerSitePark.com. Today, the park is a fascinating mix of past and present: Modern amenities like a playground and skate park beckon alongside historic landmark signage.

Riverside is one of many small towns north of Kansas City that flourished along the Missouri River. A state highway, Missouri 9, connects Riverside to Parkville in just 10 minutes. After visiting both towns, continue a half hour farther on another state highway, Missouri 45, to Weston for a memorable day spent exploring several beloved stops.

1857

Oldest Working Stagecoach Stop, Santa Fe Trail

Mahaffie Stagecoach Stop & Farm

1200 Kansas City Rd., Olathe, KS

James B. and Lucinda Mahaffie rolled into Olathe (literally—on a wagon!) from Indiana in 1857. They initially settled in downtown Olathe, building a wood-frame home that they would move (with a team of oxen) the next year to their new farmland.

The wood home was replaced by a stone residence in 1865—the stone home still stands and is part of the historic site. The Mahaffies farmed 340 acres and owned even more land throughout Johnson County and other Kansas locations. According to the historic attraction's website, "the Mahaffie farm was one of the most prosperous in Johnson County in the 1860s and early 1870s."

Not only was the Mahaffie's Olathe land optimal for farming, it was also located on the Santa Fe Trail's Westport Route, which carried travelers from Westport, Missouri, west so they could continue on the Santa Fe Trail or connect to the Oregon or California Trail. The Barlow & Sanderson Stagecoach line struck a deal with the Mahaffie family to host a stagecoach stop on their property for both passenger and mail traffic. From about 1865 to 1870, hungry travelers could fuel up with a home-cooked meal served in the farmhouse's basement kitchen and dining hall.

Courtesy of the National Park Service

James and Lucinda would retire from farming in the mid-1880s and relocate back to the Olathe city limits. Ownership of the farm changed several times in subsequent decades until the City of Olathe purchased the land and buildings in 1979 to operate them as a museum and historic site.

The site now thrives as a living history museum. Visitors can take their own wagon rides in Concord- or mudwagon-style models. Livestock, including horses, sheep, and chickens, inhabit the land just as they did centuries ago. A "newer" addition to the historic site—an Agricultural Heritage Barn, opened in 2014—showcases 19th-century farm implements and horse-drawn vehicles that are still used in farm operations today. The bustling farm is also home to a blacksmith shop, an ice house, and crop fields, a true representation of everything a late-19th-century farm would need to sustain itself and provide for others.

If your visit happens to coincide with the Fourth of July you're in luck! The Mahaffie Stagecoach Stop & Farm hosts an annual historic reenactment of one of the biggest holidays of the year for the Mahaffie family Festivities include period-specific games, a live concert, a reading of the Declaration of Independence, and more, all culminating in an 1860s-style fireworks display.

1834

Oldest Continuously Occupied Home in Kansas

The Rookery

12–14 Sumner Pl., Leavenworth, KS

Part of Fort Leavenworth (the oldest army post west of the Mississippi River, established in 1827), the Rookery holds dual historic distinctions: Built circa 1834, it's the oldest surviving building on Fort Leavenworth and is also the oldest continuously occupied home in Kansas. Past residents include General Douglas MacArthur and Andrew H. Reeder, the first governor of the Kansas Territory.

Should you decide to visit the Rookery, keep this in mind: The area's rolling terrain is part of the Glacial Hills Scenic Byway. At one time, this lush land was covered with ancient glaciers that carved hills and valleys as they slowly receded. The byway itself is filled with history, including one of the most famous Pony Express routes and two notable Kansas towns: Atchison, home of Amelia Earhart, and Troy, where Abraham Lincoln delivered an iconic campaign speech in 1859.

Fort Leavenworth's location to the northeast of Kansas City made it a bustling destination as wagon traffic in the mid-1800s passed through to continue on the Santa Fe and Oregon Trails. The fort played an important role during the Civil War and later became "the finest senior tactical school in the world for advanced military education," according to the Kansas Sampler Foundation.

Thousands of military officers come to Fort Leavenworth to earn degrees from the Command and Staff General College. That continual influx of officers and their families has helped keep the Rookery occupied, even as stories of paranormal activity within the home flourish. Melissa Bower, a reporter for the *Fort Leavenworth Lamp*, interviewed a family in 2009 about their ghostly encounters, including disappearing items, lights turning on, sounds of furniture moving, and noisy footsteps and conversation, especially at night.

If you travel to the area in early October, check dates for the annual Haunted Fort Leavenworth tour, which has previously featured the Rookery. Whatever time of year you visit Fort Leavenworth, please make sure everyone in your group has a current picture ID.

Courtesy of the Library of Congress

1875

OLDEST COWBOY BOOT IN AMERICA

HYER BOOTS

Olathe, KS

"So a cowboy walks into a cobbler's shop . . ."

No, this isn't the start of a bawdy joke; it's the opening to an incredible (and true) story. As the allure of the Wild West beckoned in the late 19th century, a cowboy prepared for his own westward adventure. His need for proper footwear took him to an Olathe cobbler shop owned by C.H. Hyer in 1875. Hyer accepted the customer's request and created the first cowboy boot.

Throughout the next few decades, word spread about Hyer's boots and orders poured in. Cattlemen and rodeo performers became some of Hyer's top customers, thanks not only to Hyer's craftsmanship but also to an innovative mail-order system. During both world wars, the fit and durability of the boots made them a popular choice for military members, including some familiar names: Teddy Roosevelt and Dwight Eisenhower. Fun fact: Marilyn Monroe was a customer, too.

Just what is it about Hyer boots that made them such a sought-after staple? Over the years, Hyer worked tirelessly to

Courtesy of Hyer Boots

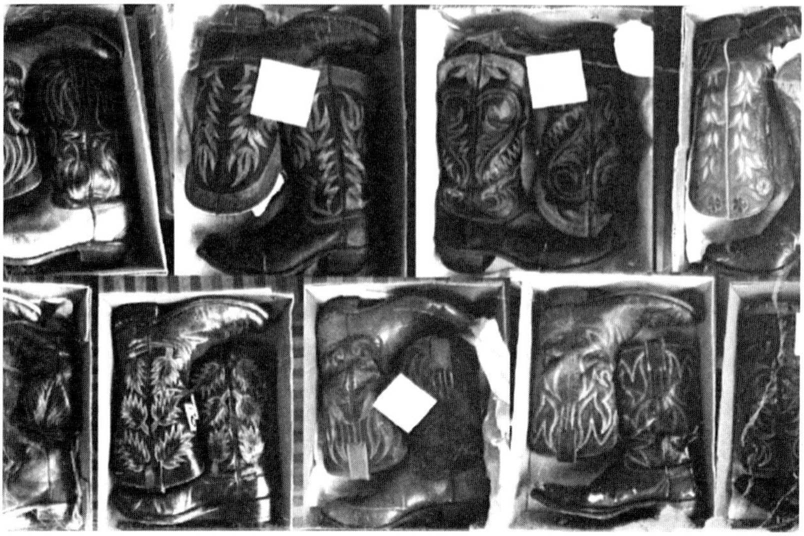

Courtesy of Hyer Boots

improve his designs, introducing features like decorative stitch patterns that are functional and eye-catching. To date, these stitch patterns remain the same used in Hyer's first decades. Leather stacked heels, leather side piping, and an oil-infused outsole combine to create a comfortable yet enduring fit that stands up to even the toughest conditions, as evidenced by Hyer's customer list.

Hyer Boots closed in the 1970s when the business succumbed to financial hardship. Then, in the 1990s, Hyer's great-great-grandson, Zach Hyer, discovered a stash of memorabilia about the family-owned business and committed to reopening it. Zach and his fiancée, Alicia, worked tirelessly over the next several years, finally relaunching Hyer Boots in 2010 with the signature Horseman & Ranch Boot.

Find Hyer Boots in several Kansas City–area retail locations, including Nigro's Western Store in Shawnee; Cavender's Western Outfitter in Kansas City, Kansas; or Buchheit in Blue Springs. Online shopping is also available—C.H. Hyer would be proud to see how his mail-order service evolved!

1975

Oldest Park in Merriam Named for a Woman

Esther Brown Memorial Park

5040 Booker St., Merriam, KS

As history unfolds, certain people play key roles in determining what lies ahead. One of those people: South Park, Kansas, resident Esther Brown.

Brown's story is concentrated in the late 1940s, but the legacy starts much earlier. Walker School, built in 1888 to house both black and white students, became an all-black school as the school district began segregating in 1900. White students were sent to newly built schools, while black students remained in the neglected one-room schoolhouse. (Note: Today, the school operates as Philadelphia Baptist Church, 9420 W 50th Terrace, Merriam, Kansas.)

When South Park Elementary School opened in 1947, black students weren't allowed to attend. Esther Brown organized

Esther and Paul Brown. Courtesy of JoCo Museum

black parents in a boycott of Walker School (dubbed "Walker's Walkouts"), and black students instead attended school in private homes under the tutelage of another educator and civil rights pioneer, Corinthian Clay Nutter.

Brown organized such a groundswell of citizen support that the battle moved to the courtroom in a local 1949 case, *Webb v. School District #90*. The case would eventually advance to the Kansas Supreme Court, which ruled in favor of admitting black children to South Park schools (and would also establish the background for the landmark 1954 *Brown v. Board of Education* lawsuit). Brown, who encouraged parents to start a local chapter of the NAACP, was elected to the Kansas State NAACP Board of Directors after her legal victory, where she contributed her successful fundraising skills to help power the Brown case (clarifying note: The plaintiff in *Brown v. Board of Education* was Oliver Brown). When the US Supreme Court ruled in favor of Brown, Esther Brown made remarks to the crowd calling out the importance of grassroots activism.

"It is the 'little people' like us who bring about such things as Monday's Supreme Court opinion," Brown said, as quoted in an article by Deborah Keating for the University of Missouri–Kansas City's Profiles in Activism. "The most brilliant lawyers couldn't have succeeded but for the help of people like you here tonight."

An exhibit created in partnership with the Johnson County Museum and South Park Elementary School recounts the struggle for equal education in South Park. The exhibit is on permanent display in Merriam Park Elementary School and was dedicated to the memory of Corinthian Clay Nutter in May 2004.

1927

Oldest Smokehouse

Fritz's Meat & Superior Sausage

10326 State Line Rd., Leawood, KS

Smoked meats can make or break a barbecue meal. Luckily, the Fritz family has spent four generations perfecting the art of smoked meat—and the longevity of their business speaks to their prowess.

Fritz and Rose Plapp opened the business's first location in 1927 in Kansas City's Midtown. Plapp, a German immigrant, prepared his products with techniques he learned in Germany. One of his nonnegotiables? No fillers—ever—used in hot dogs or sausages.

The growing business moved to their larger and current facility on State Line Road in 1969. The property includes a family butcher shop, and everything they sell is made by hand. When you visit the shop, you'll see meats smoking over natural hickory wood right in the front of the store.

As prolific local food writer and underground supper club founder Jenny Vergara wrote for *Leawood City Lifestyle*, Fritz's stocks 18 varieties of sausage ranging from knackwurst and chorizo to hot Polish sausage and competition barbecue sausage, both of which are award-winning. Feeling especially adventurous? How about alligator, ostrich, or elk sausage? Try it and report back!

Brisk business gets even crazier as Thanksgiving approaches; Fritz's sells smoked turkeys and hams and will also smoke any meat you bring them for $2 per pound (a year-round offer).

Courtesy of Martin City Telegraph

Take Vergara's advice and get lunch from Fritz's. A rotating selection of daily lunch specials showcase a variety of meats, from a half slab of St. Louis pork ribs to a Fritz's specialty: sausage burnt ends doused in barbecue sauce. Or opt for a lunchtime favorite: jalapeño cheddarwurst or regular cheddarwurst.

Good news! If you develop a love of Fritz's while you're here, don't fret when you return home. Fritz's offers nationwide shipping, so you can get your Fritz's fix as needed. Shop at fritzskcmeats.com.

1861/2001

OLDEST STATE EDUCATIONAL INSTITUTION IN KANSAS

KANSAS SCHOOL FOR THE DEAF + MUSEUM OF DEAF HISTORY, ARTS & CULTURE, INC.

450 and 455 E Park St., Olathe, KS

This entry in *Oldest Kansas City* does double duty to recognize two important Kansas landmarks.

The first is the Kansas School for the Deaf, established in October 1861 by Philip A. Emery. Emery had relocated to the area after being both student and teacher at the Indiana School for the Deaf. The school initially opened in a small home in Baldwin City, Kansas, saved from possible destruction during the Civil War, and relocated to the state capital, Topeka.

Courtesy of the Kansas School for the Deaf

Kansas School for the Deaf early football team. Courtesy of the Kansas School for the Deaf

Olathe leaders, including Senator W.H. Fishback, continued to fight for the school to move to Olathe, which it did in 1866.

The school continues to operate today and "is known for its academic excellence in pre-college preparation and its career and transition program leading to job placement upon graduation," according to the school website, kansasdeaf.gov. "The Kansas State School for the Deaf is also noted for its winning athletic teams (National Deaf Champions in football, basketball and volleyball) and still boasts of beating the University of Kansas in baseball in 1897 and 1900."

Increasing attention and recognition led to a noticeable uptick in visitors asking for details about the school and general information about deaf history, arts, and culture. A group of deaf and hearing Kansans, supported by the City of Olathe, opened the Museum of Deaf History, Arts & Culture across the street from the historic school.

A number of permanent and traveling exhibits take visitors on a fascinating and informative exploration of the deaf experience through art, interviews, and immersive interactions. The museum is also home to a small but well-stocked library focused on "anything and everything about Deaf people, their experiences, history, languages, arts and culture," according to the museum's website, museumofdeaf.org. "Identifying and tagging such educates the public on how to recognize audism [discrimination against people who are Deaf or hard of hearing] and practice being anti-audist."

Get the most out of the museum with a self-guided or docent-led tour. The private docent tours are offered in American Sign Language, and voice interpretation is available upon request. For an even deeper dive into the culture and languages of the deaf community, set aside an hour and a half for the museum's Immersive HANDS-ON Workshop, suitable for visitors of all ages.

The Kansas School for the Deaf and Museum of Deaf History, Arts & Culture are less than five minutes from downtown Olathe. Visit the City of Olathe's website, OlatheKS.gov, to download a free mobile scavenger hunt to win prizes while you explore the downtown area.

Day Trips

1907

Oldest Continuously Operating Movie Theater in the World

Plaza 1907 Cinema

209 S Main, Ottawa, KS

Cinephiles, this one's for you. Carve out a few hours during your Kansas City trip to take an hour's drive to Ottawa, Kansas, and see a movie in the world's (yes—world's) oldest continuously operating movie theater.

You wouldn't be faulted for expecting this cinematic landmark to be on the East Coast, or in Europe. Instead, the Plaza 1907 Cinema remains open for business amid the charming surroundings of downtown Ottawa. So many landmarks—including many listed in this book—suffered damage or total destruction as the result of fires. As Plaza 1907 Cinema owner Scott Zaremba explained in a 2019 Associated Press story, movie theaters were especially susceptible to fires because early films were made of flammable materials.

Since its opening on May 22, 1907, with showings of *Bad Mother*, *A Trip to the Stars on a Soap Bubble*, and *Two Wives for One Husband*, the Plaza 1907 has operated in the same location. When the *Guinness Book of World Records* investigated an application submitted by theater staff in 2017, research indicated that the Ottawa theater predated a movie house in Denmark by a mere two days. The next year, the *Guinness Book* added the Plaza 1907 to its pages as "the world's oldest operating purpose-built cinema."

These days you can catch first-run movies on one of the theater's two screens. Save time for a trip through the theater's movie museum, an assemblage of memorabilia including props and scripts that pay dual homage to the trajectories of the theater and the film industry.

Inflation, indeed! When the Plaza 1907 Cinema opened, movie tickets cost five cents and included two films and a live music performance.

Photos courtesy of Visit KS

1842

OLDEST BAR IN MISSOURI

O'MALLEY'S 1842 PUB

540 Welt St., Weston, MO

A combination of winding, narrow stairs and a rather steep ramp will guide you nearly 60 feet underground to O'Malley's 1842 Pub. As you descend the final staircase, the smell of damp earth is subtle but unmistakable as a spectacle unfolds in front of you: a narrow, limestone-walled and log-ringed room that stretches past cozy booth seating (great for date night!) and beneath a curved, arch-shaped ceiling to a well-stocked bar that fills the far end of the space.

For the best views, grab a drink at the bar, then go back up the same steps you just traveled down. A "balcony" section rings half of the bar so that you have prime views of the distinctive space and a small stage for a rotating roster of musical performers.

You might pull out your phone, prepared to text or share a photo of your surroundings, only to find you have no signal. Of course not—you're underground, in a space that previously served as the cellar of Weston Brewing Company. German immigrant John Georgian opened the brewery in 1842 under the name Royal Brewing Company, digging the spacious cellars by hand to create natural, cave-chilled storage space to house Georgian's lager.

Prohibition wreaked havoc on Weston Brewing Company and it briefly closed. Post-repeal, the brewery reopened and rotated through several owners before Michael Coakley and Corey Weinfurt purchased the 3.2-acre property in 2005.

Now, a variety of brews—including the beloved Royal Lager and O'Malley's Cream Ale—are produced in the brewery upstairs, then piped downstairs via a refrigerated line and freshly poured for thirsty patrons. A second O'Malley's bar is located one floor above the primary cellar space, a testament to the ingenuity and incredible labor that went into the creation and carving of this underground complex.

Pro tip: Weston Brewing Company, O'Malley's 1842 Pub, and the Irish-themed America Bowman Restaurant are all in the same complex. Start with some bangers and mash followed by a brewery tour before you duck underground for a happy hour to remember. Pirtle Winery is on the other side of the parking lot, so you'll have all the makings of a . . . well, spirited . . . day!

1978

OLDEST AREA WINERY

PIRTLE WINERY

505 Spring St., Weston, MO

Courtesy of Pirtle Winery

Family-owned Pirtle Winery began as so many small businesses do: in a basement. Math professor Elbert Pirtle started making wine from a cherry tree in 1978, using space in the basement of a Lutheran Evangelical Church in Weston, Missouri, to cultivate his hobby.

That hobby quickly turned into a business and grew out of its basement confines. Now, Pirtle Winery encompasses a wine-making facility and vineyards that produce upward of 40 tons of grapes annually, including Cayuga White, Seyval Blanc, Norton, Chambourcin, St. Vincent, and Concord varieties.

The church remains an integral part of Pirtle Winery. Built by German immigrants in 1867, the church now houses a first-floor wine bar and cellar and a second-floor tasting room and gift shop. If the weather cooperates, grab a seat on the winery's vine-covered patio as you savor a full range of red and white wines, as well as mead (also known as honey wine, made from fermented honey sugars and celebrated as one of the world's oldest alcoholic beverages).

Pirtle Winery remains family-owned under the helm of brothers Ross and Scott Pirtle and is part of a bustling local wine-making industry that includes several wineries located throughout the Kansas City metro, especially in Kansas City's Northland and in rural areas of Johnson County, Kansas.

An influx of German and Italian immigrants in the mid-1800s helped bring viticulture to Missouri, resulting in a booming production second only to California until Prohibition wreaked havoc on winemakers around the state. Only one Missouri winery survived Prohibition: St. Louis–based St. Stanislaus Novitiate, producer of sacramental wine.

Although Missouri viticulture hasn't reached its pre-Prohibition prominence, it has undoubtedly revived and plays a key role in bringing tourism to historic small towns like Weston and nearby Platte City.

Weston is an approximately 45-minute drive from Kansas City, and it's well worth a day trip to learn more about this small riverboat town that dates back to 1837. In 1858, Weston's population was second only to St. Louis as enterprising hemp farmers made Weston the world's foremost hemp producer.

Courtesy of Pirtle Winery

1888

Oldest-Operating Spa in Missouri

The Elms Hotel and Spa

401 Regent St., Excelsior Springs, MO

Before we dive into the fascinating history of the Elms (you'll appreciate the pun in a moment), let's learn more about the hotel's hometown, Excelsior Springs. As you can guess by the name, Excelsior Springs is the site of mineral springs first discovered in the late 1800s. Opal Mellion, daughter of a local farmer, began bathing in and drinking the bubbly spring water to try and ease her incurable tuberculosis. The early hydrotherapy worked, and Opal was eventually cured.

Not surprisingly, word of this miraculous treatment quickly spread, and people flocked to Excelsior Springs seeking relief from ailments and illnesses. The uptick in visitor traffic prompted the construction of the first Elms Hotel in 1888, which offered guests a chance to soak in relaxing mineral baths or enjoy fresh air in the surrounding gardens. Less than a decade later, a raging fire destroyed the Elms—fortunately, no one was hurt. A second hotel, opened in 1909, also succumbed to fire a year later. The third and still-operating location opened on September 7, 1912, becoming a popular destination for a wealthy clientele that included a mix of politicians, sports stars, notorious criminals

like Al Capone and "Pretty Boy" Floyd, and Missouri-born president Harry S. Truman, who secretly sought refuge in the hotel on Election Day.

Over time, the Elms has flourished, a fascinating example of both modernization and preservation. Much of the original structure remains; in fact, traveling to the hotel's lower level to use a gently circulating European lap pool or hot tub feels like the closest thing to actual time travel.

The spa is undoubtedly the star of the Elms, an indulgent sanctuary that uses water as a central theme. Before or after spa treatments, guests enjoy use of the Grotto, built in the style of a Roman bathhouse complete with dry and steam saunas, a generously sized hot tub, and an aromatherapy bar that pairs perfectly with cold plunge and steam showers.

Given the hotel's age and rich history, it's no wonder that a veritable tapestry of paranormal lore has been woven from employee and guest experiences. SyFy's *Ghost Hunters* visited the Elms to film an episode that aired in July 2013. Nightly paranormal tours are held at 9 p.m. for an additional per-person charge. After all, nothing says "sweet dreams" like the possibility of a ghostly sighting.

Pro tip: If you feel like a splurge, book a room or suite on the Elms' fifth floor for "The Royal Treatment." Among the highlights: daily happy hour in the wood-paneled concierge lounge that offers plenty of plush seating, the perfect way to unwind before you head to dinner.

1913/2005

OLDEST CAROUSEL IN KANSAS CITY

C.W. PARKER CAROUSEL MUSEUM

320 S Esplanade St., Leavenworth, KS

When is the last time you rode a carousel—if ever? Inside Leavenworth's C.W. Parker Carousel Museum, not only will you learn the history of this amusement park staple, but you'll have a chance to ride a fully restored and operational 1913 carousel that was originally made in Leavenworth.

You'll also learn more about Charles Wallace Parker, an Illinois native who moved to Abilene, Kansas, with his family when he was five. As Parker grew up, he couldn't shake a fascination with amusement devices and rides, and so he dedicated his career to them. His first investment: a portable shooting gallery, purchased with money he saved while working as a janitor.

He turned his attention to carousels after spending many of his hard-earned dollars so that his daughter could ride one outside of the grocery store at five cents per ride. He built his first carousel in 1892 and continued creating carousels (or carry-us-alls) that were designed and built to be portable.

After a property dispute in Abilene in 1911, Parker relocated the C.W. Parker Amusement Company to Leavenworth. There he created more grandiose carousel horses and added other animals as carousel mounts. A bit of trivia: The carousel you can ride at the museum is the only Parker carousel to feature two hand-carved rabbits as mounts.

The "Amusement King," as Parker came to be known, survived supply shortages caused by World War I and continued to modify his designs, eventually switching to aluminum horses (much easier to maintain). When Parker died in 1932, his son took over the company's operations in Leavenworth until 1955. In fact, you can see Paul's work in a 1950s aluminum carousel also on display at the museum, along with the oldest primitive carousel in the US.

For a mere $6 you can enjoy a 90-minute guided tour through the museum and a carousel ride. The museum is open from 1 to 5 p.m., Saturdays and Sundays, and closed during the month of January

---

Photos courtesy of the C. W. Parker Carousel Museum

2013

Oldest Collection of Woven Silk Tapestries in Missouri

National Silk Art Museum

423 Main St., Weston, MO

Who knew that you could have a drink in Missouri's oldest bar and examine the world's most extensive collection of woven silk tapestries in the same town? Welcome to Weston!

The museum itself is one of the newer destinations in this book. Owner John Pottie opened the museum in a former bank in 2013, giving his rapidly growing collection of woven silk tapestries a new home. Previously, they had been on display in Pottie's German restaurant, also in Weston.

How did Pottie cultivate such an extensive collection? As he recounted in a Flatland KC story written by Cami Koons and Catherine Hoffman, it all started with a trip to an antique mall. Pottie bid $50 on a print that caught his eye, depicting a lively billiards game. When Pottie tried to frame the print, "he discovered the detailed billiards scene he'd bought was, in fact, a woven piece of silk. Inspired by the unusual find, Pottie visited libraries and museums looking for information on the piece and the art form. He came away empty-handed. It seemed no one knew anything about the silk art piece he'd stumbled upon."

He dedicated the next 40-plus years of his life to research, much of it done without the Internet. By amassing a collection of silk pieces purchased from art galleries, auctions, and antique malls, Pottie learned not only about the general art of silk weaving, but also about the pioneering techniques and machines that made this art form possible. One example is the Jacquard loom, which, according to the museum's website, "started a technological revolution in the textile industry. The system of punch cards used in its operation became a prototype for the first mechanical computers" and would later become a key component of the first IBM computers.

Intricate tapestries on display at the museum showcase work of mostly French and English artists spanning the 15th through 20th centuries, and a rotating selection of traveling exhibits feature themed displays that offer an even deeper dive into a particular period, technique, or style.

The National Silk Art Museum is located in downtown Weston, making it part of a rewarding day spent exploring this fascinating riverfront town. Museum hours as of this book's publication are 10 a.m. to 4 p.m., Wednesday through Saturday

---

OLDEST DAIRY FARM

SHATTO MILK COMPANY

9406 MO-33, Osborn, MO

You can't write a book about Cowtown and not talk about dairy farming! Shatto Milk Company—or, more accurately, the family-owned farming enterprise that eventually launched the dairy business—began in the late 1800s when Minnie Porter married George Winstead and they bought the land in Clinton County that's still farmed today.

The family grew, and descendants of Minnie and George began exploring their own paths. Two of their children remained to run the family farm: Mary Alice and Jack. Their sister, Georgia, married Ivan Cox and returned to the farm, where Ivan and Mary Alice began operating a dairy.

Georgia and Ivan had three children starting in the late 1940s. One of their daughters, Barbara, would later marry Leroy Shatto. And it was Barbara and Leroy who took over the farm when Ivan retired in the mid-1980s.

As the calendar rolled into the 1990s, dairy farms throughout the area struggled to maintain operations because of low prices paid by dairy cooperatives. The Shattos fought a similar battle, realizing in the mid-'90s that the farm couldn't sustain itself.

Minnie Porter and George Winstead. Courtesy of Shatto Milk Company

Courtesy of Shatto Milk Company

In 2001, Leroy and Barbara decided to bypass the dairy cooperative and bottle their own milk, which they would supply directly to customers in Kansas City and St. Joseph. On June 4, 2003, Shatto Milk Company delivered its first supply of locally made and bottled milk to around 10 retail stores throughout Kansas City.

Today, Shatto Milk is easily found in grocery stores and markets around the metro. The glass milk bottles require a deposit, factored into the retail price. Customers can return clean, empty glass bottles and have their deposits refunded. Shatto also offers a robust home-delivery program that will drop fresh milk, groceries, and gifts at your doorstep.

Part of Shatto Milk's appeal is their commitment to creativity and local pride. They've introduced an adventurous range of flavored milks to store shelves, including cotton candy, root beer, and banana. They also release limited-edition flavors, like salted caramel, to celebrate historic Kansas City Chiefs wins (there have been a few of those recently). And they've expanded to include a full range of locally made dairy goods, including cheese, cheese curds, butter, and ice cream.

If your schedule allows, the hour-ish drive to the Shatto farm is well worth it. Reach out in advance to book a farm tour (shattomilk.com) to learn how exactly Shatto Milk gets from their farm to your table. Or keep an eye on their events calendar for annual traditions like Family Day at the Farm and the Holiday Open House.

1808

OLDEST MILITARY FORT

FORT OSAGE

105 Osage St., Sibley, MO

As Meriwether Lewis and William Clark set off on their famous exploration along the Missouri River at the behest of President Thomas Jefferson, they added a number of landmarks and moments to the historic legacies of both Missouri and Kansas.

In 1808, Clark and Captain Eli B. Clemson led soldiers in building Fort Osage a little over 30 miles northeast of Kansas City on a bluff overlooking the Missouri River, a location that offered a clear view for miles. The fort served several purposes, functioning "as an outpost in the newly acquired Louisiana Purchase, housing soldiers to guard the new territory, and protecting the U.S. Factory Trade House," according to a brochure created by the National Park Service. "Fort Osage also aided the American government in befriending the area's Osage Indians. Finally, the Fort offered Missouri's early settlers and explorers a sanctuary from which to venture westward."

Both traders and soldiers had abandoned the fort by 1827 after successful lobbying by private traders to end the Fur Trade Factory System, which had given the federal government control over the fur trade.

"The factory system began as an attempt to eliminate the worst excesses of the fur trade by prohibiting alcohol sales and providing goods to [Indigenous peoples] at wholesale prices," according to the Wisconsin Historical Society.

Despite the fort's closing after a relatively short tenure, people throughout Kansas City and beyond quickly took interest in it. Historic designations began in 1909, when the

Daughters of the American Revolution built a Santa Fe Trail monument on the southeast edge of Sibley Cemetery. They would later install a nearby memorial tablet in 1926.

According to documentation on the Fort Osage Historic Landmark website, 1940 proved a pivotal year for the fort. Author Kate Gregg published "The History of Fort Osage" in the *Missouri Historical Review*, which the Fort Osage website calls, "the most important publication on the history of the fort." In promoting her work, Dr. Gregg spoke to the Native Sons of Kansas City and strongly recommended that the fort be reconstructed.

Jackson County purchased land surrounding the fort, establishing Fort Osage as one of the earliest county parks. Reconstruction began in earnest in the late 1940s and would continue until 1961. In the 1980s the park evolved to become a living history museum, giving visitors a more authentic experience of life in and around Fort Osage.

Sibley is a roughly 40-minute drive from downtown Kansas City and Fort Osage is 14 miles northeast of Independence. Set off in the morning to spend a few hours exploring Fort Osage, then enjoy dinner at one of the many restaurants around the historic Independence Square.

SOURCES

Oldest Barbecue Restaurant: kcur.org/arts-life/2021-02-13/kansas-city-barbecue-bbq-henry-perry-gates-arthur-bryants-history

Oldest Collection of Victorian Homes: northeastnews.net/pages/pendleton-heights

Oldest Farmers Market: thecitymarketkc.org/wp-content/uploads/2018/03/river-market_booklet_2009_sm.pdf

Oldest Operating Black-Owned Radio Station: aahtkc.org/kprs

Oldest Original Pork Tenderloin Sandwich Recipe: kcur.org/arts-life/2018-08-31/the-story-behind-a-unique-pork-tenderloin-in-kansas-city

Oldest Skyscraper: hmdb.org/m.asp?m=64003

Oldest Black-Owned Brewery in Missouri: aahtkc.org/18thandvine; kcur.org/arts-life/2023-06-30/kansas-citys-newest-brewery-isnt-just-the-first-in-missouri-owned-by-african-americans-its-sacred-soil

Oldest Active Black-Owned Newspaper: aahtkc.org/kansascitycall

Oldest East–West Boulevard: arcadiapublishing.com/products/9781467112598?srsltid=AfmBOop-62CFBaH2Ldu9q_LemRFpphgkw-6mguaeSgyEfkNrRmXFe0eWXs

Oldest Operating Retail Business: kcur.org/arts-life/2022-03-17/brownes-irish-marketplace-in-kansas-city-turns-135-it-reminds-us-of-what-we-grew-up-with

Oldest and Largest Collection of Pre–Civil War Artifacts: 1856.com/about-the-museum; visitkc.com/business-detail/arabia-steamboat-museum

Oldest Museum Building in Kansas City: kansascity.com/news/your-kcq/article248281990.html; kclibrary.org/events/kansas-city-place-time; kcur.org/arts-life/2021-10-14/it-took-7-years-and-over-a-thousand-hands-to-restore-the-kansas-city-museum

Oldest Fried-Chicken Restaurant: kcur.org/arts-life/2021-12-19/kansas-city-cinnamon-rolls; stroudskc.com/history/; fox4kc.com/mornings/recipes-strouds-pan-fried-chicken

Oldest-Remaining Wagon Tracks: kclibrary.org/events/kansas-city-place-time; nps.gov/places/000/minor-park.htm

Oldest Museum of Barbecue: news.visitkc.com/releases/worlds-first-museum-of-bbq-is-opening-in-kansas-city-in-2025; AmericanRoyal.com

Oldest Golf Course: martincitytelegraph.com/2019/08/27/kansas-citys-first-country-club-was-far-from-par-for-the-course/; jchs.org/jchs-e-journal/janssenplace; kcparks.org/places/gillham-park

Oldest Antebellum Home: wornallmajors.org/explore/majors-house/; wornallmajors.org/walk

Oldest Building in Kansas City: kellyswestportinn.com/history

Oldest Baseball League Formed in Kansas City: aahtkc.org/nlbm

Oldest Steak House: goldenoxkc.com/about

Oldest Happy Meal: fox4kc.com/news/man-who-created-happy-meals-looks-back-on-60-years-in-kansas-city

Oldest Science-Focused Library: lindahall.org/about/our-story

Oldest Continuously Operating Jazz Club in the US: aahtkc.org/mutualmusicians-foundation; historicmissouri.org/items/show/146; atlasobscura.com/places/mutual-musicians-foundation-kansas-city

Oldest Black Church: secondbaptistkcmo.org/images/SBC_History_160.pdf; kcur.org/show/up-to-date/2013-08-09/kansas-citys-first-black-baptist-church-marks-150-year-anniversary; FOSSKC.org

Oldest Time Period Represented by a Living History Museum: shoalcreeklivinghistorymuseum.com/history-of-shoal-creek.html

Oldest Fine-Dining Restaurant: trumanlibrary.gov/education/student-resources/places/kansas-city/savoy-grill; kansascity.com/living/food-drink/article281400283.html

Oldest Local Apartment Buildings Designed by a Woman: digital.shsmo.org/digital/collection/mhr/id/44123?_gl=1*18w8qft*_ga*NjA2NDEyMjgzLjE3NDgwMTkzMDQ.*_ga_2ERXEH2DGZ*czE3NDgwMTkzMDQkbzEkZzAkdDE3NDgwMTkzMDQkajAkbDAkaDA

Oldest LGBTQ Bar: libweb.umkc.edu/content/images/glama/timeline/jackson-book-bar-list.pdf; kcrainbowtour.com

Oldest Area Cemetery: kshb.com/news/local-news/a-place-in-time-book-takes-a-look-back-to-historic-kansas-city-sites

Oldest Local Distillery: jriegerco.com/history/about-us; inc.com/brit-morse/andy-rieger-whiskey-distillery-historic-kansas-city-brand.html

Oldest Woman-Built Event Space: midtownkcpost.com/drexel-hall-built-by-shrewd-businesswoman-has-seen-a-century-of-history

Oldest Continuously Operating Fountain: kcparks.org/places/womens-leadership-fountain

Oldest Studio Where Walt Disney Worked: kcur.org/history/2021-05-22/walt-disney-didnt-actually-draw-mickey-mouse-meet-the-kansas-city-artist-who-did; thankyouwaltdisney.org

Oldest Glass Curtain Wall Architecture: tss-bulletproof.com/blog/introduction-glass-curtain-wall; helixus.com/project/andrews-mcmeel-universal

Oldest Brick House: aahtkc.org/harriskearneyhouse; westporthistoricalkc.org; martincitytelegraph.com/2024/07/19/reopening-the-story-of-our-history-the-1855-harris-kearney-house

Oldest Existing Ballroom: pendergastkc.org/local-subjects/el-torreon-dance-hall

Oldest Synagogue: synagoguesofthesouth.cofc.edu/synagogues/kansas-city-mo-congregation-bnai-jehudah-1908/; kshb.com/news/local-news/a-place-in-time-book-takes-a-look-back-to-historic-kansas-city-sites

Oldest Continuously Operating Men's Clothier: michaelsclothing.com/Home/History

Oldest World War I Memorial in the US: theworldwar.org/explore/our-story

Oldest Midwestern Film Walk of Fame: flatlandkc.org/curiouskc/kansas-city-film-row-links-crossroads-arts-district-to-hollywood; umkc.edu/news/posts/2022/june/clio-app-puts-local-history-on-a-national-stage.html

Oldest and Largest Collection of Fine-Scale Miniatures: toyandminiaturemuseum.org/about

Oldest Jazz Memorabilia on Display: aahtkc.org/americanjazzmuseum; aahtkc.org/greenbook

Oldest Watering Hole and Campground: kcjc.com/index.php/current-news/latest-news/5911-local-jewish-family-completes-land-gift-to-jackson-county; cavespring.org

Oldest Living Bur Oak Tree: flatlandkc.org/curiouskc/big-tree-a-living-monument-in-old-northeast; www2.ljworld.com/news/2002/mar/26/storm_toppled_historic

Oldest Airline Museum in Kansas City: twamuseum.org/about; airlinehistory.org/aircraft/twa-moonliner

Oldest Local Hospital to Treat Black Patients: aahtkc.org/wheatleyprovidenthospital

Oldest North–South Boulevard: kchistory.org/image/paseo-north-17th-street-0; arcadiapublishing.com/products/9781467112598?srsltid=AfmBOoo8lkxLQOhrqVcBC5hKdHFNWDQESTwzYPN10n6l7WYt8r14lByd

Oldest Still-Operating Mexican Restaurant: eater.com/2019/4/23/18294269/kansas-city-tacos-origin-parmesan; loscorralskc.com

Oldest Private Cemetery: visitkansascityks.com/listing/wyandot-national-burying-ground/58/; kcur.org/show/central-standard/2014-10-29/the-story-behind-the-historic-american-indian-cemetery-in-downtown-kck; theclio.com/entry/143064

Oldest Home in Wyandotte County: grinterfriends.com/; travelks.com/listing/grinter-place-state-historic-site/1460; kansashistory.gov/p/grinter-place/20759

Oldest Privately Owned Bowling Alley: flatlandkc.org/arts-culture/let-the-good-times-roll-at-st-johns-catholic-club/; imdb.com/title/tt10662296

Oldest Queen-Anne-Mansion-Turned-Museum: kcur.org/show/central-standard/2015-09-22/why-pope-john-paul-iis-airplane-bed-is-in-kansas-city-kansas; strawberryhillmuseum.org/owners

Oldest Remnants of the Underground Railroad: civilwaronthewesternborder.org/encyclopedia/quindaro-kansas; QuindaroRuinsProjectFoundationKCK.org; urbanhikeskc.com

Oldest Continuously Running Festival: kcrenfest.com/about-us

Oldest Soda Fountain to Employ Harry S. Truman: clintonssodafountain.com/; hmdb.org/m.asp?m=34789; trumanlibrary.gov/education/student-resources/trumans-early-jobs/drugstore-clerk-at-14

Oldest Government Building in Jackson County: independencemo.gov/visitors/our-history-and-culture/1827-log-courthouse; theclio.com/entry/10673; visitkc.com/business-detail/1827-log-courthouse

Oldest Family-Owned Restaurant: gkcur.org/show/central-standard/2015-11-13/independence-diner-serves-up-chili-from-century-old-recipe; thepitchkc.com/dixons-famous-chili-legacy-crosses-everything-from-tacos-to-truman

Oldest Burger Joint: kcur.org/arts-life/2024-12-21/oldest-restaurants-kansas-city-barbecue-history

Oldest Victorian Mansion: vailemansion.org/history; jchs.org/jchs-e-journal/2023/3/15/gilded-age-splendor-of-vaile-mansion-endures-into-21-st-century

Oldest Area Jail: jchs.org/plan-your-visit; jchs.org/1859jailmuseum; martincitytelegraph.com/2024/08/11/inside-the-history-of-the-1859-jail-museum

Oldest Private College or University: jewell.edu/about/jewell-history; hjseries.org

Oldest Bed-and-Breakfast: mainstreetinn-parkville.com/missouri-bed-and-breakfas/; visitmo.com/places-to-stay/main-street-inn-parkville; facebook.com/parkuniversity/posts/do-you-know-about-old-kate/10153162209032349

Oldest-Known Bank Robbed in Daylight, Peacetime: visitclaymo.com/business/jesse-james-bank-museum; missourilife.com/february-13-1866-2; visitlibertymo.com/Blog.aspx?IID=77&ARC=121

Oldest Local Home of the Hopewell Culture: rennerbrennersitepark.com/; theclio.com/entry/150566; britannica.com/topic/Hopewell-culture; riversidemo.gov/community/city_history.php

Oldest Working Stagecoach Stop, Santa Fe Trail: nps.gov/places/mahaffie-stagecoach-stop-farm-historic-site.htm; mahaffie.org/about-us

Oldest Continuously Occupied Home in Kansas: visitleavenworthks.com/visitors/page/rookery; kansassampler.org/8wondersofkansas-history/historic-fort-leavenworth; army.mil/article/28851/family_has_unusual_experiences_living_in_a_haunted_house

Oldest Cowboy Boot in America: hyerboots.com/pages/about-us?srsltid=AfmBOoo-iN-FXMKy89VeleF6iB3YfFzVN7yCCdfzpK-ZAh-ZxQDwqLaoQB; kansascitymag.com/american-royal-and-kcs-hyer-boots-create-a-limited-edition-cowboy-boot

Oldest Park in Merriam Named for a Woman: merriam.org/Government/Departments/Parks-Rec/Parks/Brown-Memorial-Park; info.umkc.edu/kcactivism/?page_id=259#:~:text=Esther%20Brown%20was%20instrumental%20in,Kansas%2C%20and%20the%20Webb%20v

Oldest Smokehouse: citylifestyle.com/articles/fritzs-meats-and-superior-sausage

Oldest State Educational Institution in Kansas: kansasdeaf.gov/history; museumofdeaf.org/about

Oldest Continuously Operating Movie Theater in the World: travelks.com/listing/plaza-cinema-movie-and-memorabilia-museum/3655; atlasobscura.com/places/plaza-1907-cinema; cjonline.com/story/news/local/2019/08/24/ottawa-boasts-worlds-oldest-continuously-operating-movie-theater/4388643007

Oldest Bar in Missouri: savingplaces.org/stories/omalleys-pub-historic-bar; atlasobscura.com/places/omalleys-pub

Oldest Area Winery: pirtlewinery.com/our-story; columbiamissourian.com/special_section/tourism/northwest_missouri/pirtle-winery-producing-wine-and-mead-in-weston-for-44-years/article_66fa2ee4-c997-11ec-b7eb-e7496734a986.html

Oldest-Operating Spa in Missouri: elmshotelandspa.com/elms-history.htm; visitexcelsior.com/excelsior-history

Oldest Carousel in Kansas City: visitleavenworthks.com/visitors/page/cw-parker-carousel-museum-gift-shop; travelks.com/listing/c-w-parker-carousel-museum/1578

Oldest Collection of Woven Silk Tapestries in Missouri: flatlandkc.org/arts-culture/theres-a-jewel-hidden-in-weston; nationalsilkartmuseum.com

Oldest Dairy Farm: shattomilk.com/history

Oldest Military Fort: nps.gov/places/fort-osage-mo.htm; fortosagenhs.com/history

Vaile Mansion in Independence, Missouri
Courtesy of Visit KC

INDEX